Charles Bulkley

Catechetical Exercises

Charles Bulkley

Catechetical Exercises

ISBN/EAN: 9783743406858

Manufactured in Europe, USA, Canada, Australia, Japa

Cover: Foto ©ninafisch / pixelio.de

Manufactured and distributed by brebook publishing software (www.brebook.com)

Charles Bulkley

Catechetical Exercises

By CHARLES BULKLEY.

Ἡνικα δει ειπειν λογον, ȣ κατα το μαρτυριον μονον, αλλα γαρ και τον και' ερωτησιν και αποκρισιν.
  Clement. Alex. Strom. L. vi.

Be sure to teach your children with all the sweetness and gentleness you can; lest if you should be severe, and over-task them, religion should seem to them rather a burden than a blessing.
        BISHOP KEN.

And thou shalt teach them diligently unto thy children, and shalt TALK of them. MOSES.

LONDON:
Printed for J. JOHNSON, in St. Paul's Church-Yard.

MDCCLXXIV.

PREFACE.

THE author of the following sheets has always considered himself as being accountable both to God and his fellow-creatures for the use that he makes of his time, and of any slender powers he may be possessed of: and, if he be not much mistaken, always carries about with him a brotherly and cordial affection towards human kind. and it is upon this principle that he has ventured them abroad; hoping that they may possibly be of some use towards suggesting a method of catechetical instruction that may at least have its advantages among the rest for the improvement of younger minds. he would by no means depreciate from the well known performances of others in this department:

PREFACE.

nor even allows himself to imagine, that those which may perhaps seem to some to be too childish even for children themselves, must needs be without their use. he cannot however but be of opinion that in one period or another of early life this mode of instruction should be so conducted, as to be to the pupil himself an exercise of his own rational and mental powers, and not merely a declaration of what others have to say. this has too much the air of authoritie; and too great a tendencie towards leading the younger sort into an apprehension, that religion has no other foundation than that of venerable custom and parental discipline. and though it may serve to awe their minds for the present, it is well if afterwards it have not a very different effect. especially if in the very manner of proceding upon these occasions a certain severe and rigid form be too strictly adhered to. to prevent which, and in order to give to
this

PREFACE.

this exercise a more chearful, manly and sociable appearance, it should be permitted sometimes at least, to intermingle itself with the other religious offices belonging to a family; and with some more general addresses upon a topic of this nature; and, as apt occasion may offer, in some sort, and in a more transient way, into freer conversation. by this means a way will be made for those other catechetical treatises not so immediately calculated for the initiatory discipline. such I mean as those of OSTERVALD, USHER, BAXTER, HAMMOND. treatises of this kind have certainly their distinct use, all else being as nearly alike as may be, as at little intervals of leisure, or upon particular occasions they may more readily and profitably be consulted. besides that in writings of this construction, there is a natural tendency to lead the reader into that most useful practice of soliloquy and self-examination, which, where there is any thing

of

PREFACE.

of a serious turn, will be apt in the perusal of them to steal upon him ere he is aware. in the mean while, some of our smaller catechisms may be made occasionally to accompany some such plan of instruction as that we have in the following lectures exhibited. and the author has only here to add, that he has such a thorough conviction of the high importance and sovereign excellency of religion, that should they but in the least degree contribute to the promoting of its influence, he shall think himself well rewarded for the publication.

ERRATA.

ERRATA.

Page 46, l. 14, for *is*, read *are.* p. 174, l. 23, *dele* the inverted comma. p. 188, l. 5. *note*, for *elifcimus*, read *difcimus*. p. 202, l. 24, after *character*, a full stop. p. 203, l. 1. *dele* now. p. 244, l. 20, after *heightned*, an interrogation. p. 251, l. 2, before *seeking*, read *the*. p. 267, l. 5, after *contemplations*, comma.

CATECHETICAL EXERCISES.

LECTURE I.

WE are now in purfuance of a defign, of which fome general account has been already given, to enter upon fuch a confideration of the grounds and principles of religion, as may, it is hoped, be efpecially ufeful towards leading the younger part of our focietie into a juft and becoming fenfe of it; and contribute at the fame time towards impreffing the minds of all with more affecting and lively apprehenfions of it's nature and importance. a capacitie for religion is the diftinguifhing excel-

LECT. I. excellencie of human nature, it is that by which we rise in eminence of being above the brute creation. whatever other traces of reason may be thought apparent in any of these; it is man alone among all the inhabitants on this earthly globe, that has it in his power to be religious. now to know and worship, to contemplate and rejoice in, to imitate and obey the great author of our being, this is religion. such then the high and glorious employment, for which we are by nature fitted. such the privileges even of our present being; which thankfully embraced and duly improved, will terminate ere long in the complete felicitie of heaven itself. yet how small and inconsiderable a share has religion

Education. in the education of our children and of our youth. if it makes any part at all of it, and be not absolutely discarded, with what carelesness and superficial formalitie is it treated, as if among all the branches of education it was by far the meanest and most insignificant. and then in after life that ignorance in every thing relative to religion, that is so justly to be imputed to the gross and shameful negligence of a parent, is usually ascribed to the stupiditie, dullness dullnefs and perverfenefs of nature. fo Lect. I. readie are we in this, as in fo many other inftances befides, rather to throw the blame upon God than upon ourfelves. But why muft it be thought a thing incredible, that even children fhould be capable of under-ftanding the principles and duties of reli-gion? if it be a capacitie at all belonging to man as fuch, it muft needs be originally inherent in our minds when children, and want only to be properly cultivated and educed and in due time put upon it's natural exer-cife and ufe. parents think their children well enough capable of underftanding the dutie, which they are owing to themfelves, Filial duty. and are apt to be fomewhat angry with them, if they appear not to do fo. why then fhould they be thought unable to form the proper notion or idea of that, which is owing from them to their heavenly father? it confifts in the very fame kind of obligations, though infinitely heightened according to the infinite tranfcendencie of that fovereign being, who is the object of it. and even the foundation of thefe duties they may furely underftand, were their thoughts but properly directed that way in the one cafe as well as in the other. a child very

Lect. I. very soon comes to apprehend that he is in some manner or another indebted to a parent for his being. may he not be made sensible that in a much stricter sense he has derived it from God? he soon comes to know that his father and mother have an authoritie over him, and have a right to command him. would it not be easie for a parent to lay hold upon this conviction in such a manner as to lead him into the rational apprehension, that God must have a still higher authoritie over him, and a still superior right to his obedience? how soon does a child, that has not very early indeed been corrupted, come to be persuaded, that he ought to love his parents on account of the blessings and benefits he has received from them? and can it be a matter of any great difficultie to convince him that he is under far higher obligations to the goodness and care of that sovereign deity who made him? these reasonings and illustrations I have introduced as a kind of specimen of the manner in which the subject we have proposed to treat upon, may be adapted to the capacities of children; and yet this in perfect consistencie with the rational grounds of religion in itself. for the

the stronger and more forcible any reason- *Lect. I.*
ing, so much the more easily is it to be
discerned by every capacitie. so that reli- *Capacitie.*
gion being founded upon the plainest and
most convincing arguments, upon the
strongest and most demonstrative reasonings, must on that account be so much the
more easily inculcated in the rational nature of it, even upon the young and tender
mind. you see what a copious subject we
have undertaken; a subject in which those
of all parties are alike concerned. since it
is by the first and fundamental principles of
religion that all particular controversies are
to be decided; and were there no sufficient
foundation for religion in the general nature and idea of it, all our partie disputes
must be at an end of course. but more particularly still, as to the subjects we propose
to treat of; they are first, a deitie, his being, his attributes, his providence; and *Topics.*
with respect to this last it's realitie, it's nature as a plan of moral government, it's
extent, it's views. secondly, man, his
origin, his nature, his connexions, the end
of his creation, his happiness, his duties,
his present situation, natural and moral;
and his character in general. thirdly, a
future

LECT. I. future state; and the hope and expectations of mankind in relation to it. fourthly, the christian religion, it's design, it's evidences, principles, usefulness and duties. in treating upon the several topics of religion as founded in reason and nature I shall take frequent occasion to illustrate them by the language and maxims of the scriptures, tho' their authoritie and evidence come not till afterwards distinctly to be considered. in the mean time by this manner of proceding, we shall have as we go along, and before we touch directly upon that particular, one considerable argument in favor of the scriptures, namely, their harmony and agreement with natural religion; a point so considerable indeed, that were it wanting, nothing could be sufficient to establish their authoritie, nor any other reasonings whatsoever amount to a proper and satisfactorie evidence in favor of them. and as to the duties in particular of religion, I shall shew how they arise out of each truth or principle of it as I go along. and as one and the same dutie has oftentimes a foundation in several different truths or principles of religion, these distinct grounds of that particular dutie will be pointed out

under

under each. after which a summarie of thoſe duties, according to all the united force of obligation derived from theſe ſeveral principles, may we apprehend with the moſt proprietie, and advantage be introduced.

As religion has ſuch an ample and ſtrong foundation in truth and nature, we cannot but conclude, that effects of a proportionable kind, and in the higheſt degree conducing to the good of mankind would ariſe from the profeſſion of it, were ſuch a profeſſion attended with proper ideas, and diſtinct conceptions of it's nature and importance in the mind. but here lies our grand defect; and the reaſon why we ſee ſo little either of the love, or of the fruits of religion; and why there is ſo little zeal among us either for its puritie or its prevalencie, is that we give ſo little attention to it's fundamental principles, and to thoſe reaſons, which are with ſuch force and evidence to be aſſigned in favor of it. but here, whilſt we are talking of religion and making mention of that deitie, whoſe being is the ground, and whoſe perfections are the object of it, ſome of thoſe children perhaps, whoſe intereſt in this deſign I have ſo much at heart, may be ready to aſk, ·

"but

LECT. I. "but where is the God you speak of, a
"God my maker? I have often *heard of*
"*him with the hearing of the ear*; I have
"heard my parents talk of such a being;
"and on a certain day of every week I
"hear much discoursed of concerning
"him: but methinks I should be extremely
"glad if mine eye could see him; and, if
"I cannot see him, how is it that I am
"to be made sensible that there is such
"a being? why, pray, my dear child,
"did you ever see the king? no. but
"you believe, I suppose, that there is a
"king of England? yes, sir, I have no
"doubt of that. why then, may you not
"reasonably believe that there is a God,
"though you have never seen him? I can-
"not say, sir, that I am altogether satis-
"fied with your argument; because, tho'
"I have not myself ever seen the king,
"I have heard of, and been in company
"of those that have seen him, but I never
"heard of, or have met with any one
"that has seen God. nay, I have been
Deitie in- "told that no body *can see him*; and I have
visible. "read the same in the bible. but pray,
"did you ever hear of any body that had
"seen the wind, that often makes such a
"rustling

" ruſtling noiſe in the ſtreets, that raiſes
" the duſt of the ground aloft into the air,
" and ſometimes ſhakes the very houſes in
" which we ſit; and yet you believe that
" there is ſuch a thing as the wind, and
" that there are a great many events
" and accidents to be aſcribed to it, tho'
" neither you nor any one elſe have ſeen
" it. indeed, ſir, I cannot ſay that I am
" quite ſatisfied yet. why ſo? becauſe,
" tho' I never *ſaw* the wind, yet I often
" *hear* it; and that convinces me as much
" that there is ſuch a thing, as if it were
" to be the object of my ſight; but of
" God I muſt ſay, that I have not *heard*
" *his voice at any time*, any more than *ſeen*
" *his ſhape*. why then, my dear child, let
" me aſk you, did you ever think? O yes.
" I am always thinking about ſomething
" or another. but do you apprehend
" that there is any man or woman in the
" world that can *ſee* you think, or *hear*
" you think? no; that is impoſſible. but
" yet you would look upon it to be very
" ſtrange, if any bodie ſhould deny that
" there was ſuch a thinking being in the
" world as you, becauſe they could neither
" *ſee*, nor *hear* your thoughts. Indeed, I
" ſhould

LECT. I. "should imagine him to be quite mad and
"out of his wits. If you then can think
"without being *seen* or *heard* to think, can
"you not easily suppose, that there may be
"some other thinking being, that neither
"you nor any one else can *see* with the
"*bodily* eye? for, tho' you have a body,
"yet your thoughts are no more to be
"seen, than if you had no body at all. (*a*)
"your thoughts therefore, and your think-
"ing power are quite distinct from your
"bodie. you can then surely apprehend,
"that there may be some thinking being
"existing, that has not a bodie, because
"you plainly perceive that it is not with
"your bodie that you yourself do think.
"as it is not therefore your bodie that
"thinks, there may be some other think-
"ing being that has no bodie; and, if a
"thinking being may be without a bodie,
                                    "then

(*a*) Est, est profecto illa vis (scil. divina): neque in his corporibus atque in hac imbecillitate nostra inest quiddam, quod vigeat & sentiat, & non est in hoc tanto naturæ tam præclaro motu. nisi forte idcirco esse non putant, quia non *apparet* nec *cernitur:* perinde quasi *nostram* ipsam *mentem*, qua sapimus, qua providemus, qua ipsa hæc agimus, ac dicimus, videre, aut plane, qualis aut ubi sit, sentire possimus. *Ciceron.* pro *Milone.*

"then it can be no objection to your be-
"lieving in such a being, that you cannot
"*see* him. but, tho' I cannot *see* God,
"yet should I not have some proof in one
"way or another given me of his being,
"before I admit that belief of it? why?
"can you not take your parents word for
"it? have they not often told you,
"that God sees you and hears you, and
"knows you and made you, and can bless
"you? and is not that enough to induce
"you to believe these things? indeed, sir,
"I apprehend that my father and mother
"would not believe them, if they had
"not some *argument* or *reason* in their own
"minds, upon which they ground that
"belief. and as I am a being of the same
"nature with them, I think that I may
"be capable at least gradually and in time,
"and having it once and again proposed
"to me, to perceive the force of this ar-
"gument. and I fancie too that I should
"be better satisfied in believing that there
"is a God, by discerning in my own mind,
"and by the exercise of my own thoughts,
"the reason of that belief, than by believ-
"ing it merely upon the word of my
"parents. besides, tho' I might depend
"upon

LECT. I.
Implicit faith.

"upon what my parents say, yet perhaps
"every bodie will not. and methinks I
"should be quite ashamed, were any one
"to ask me, why I believed that there was
"a God, and I could give no other reason,
"than because my father and my mother
"told me there was such a being. why
"should you be ashamed of that? because
"I am a reasonable creature; and I think
"it must be a shame for a reasonable crea-
"ture to believe any thing without a rea-
"son. I remember too to have read in the
"bible, that we should be *readie to give an*
"*answer to every man that may ask of us a*
"*reason of the hope that is in us.* that must
"mean, to be sure, a proper, that is, a
"rational answer, or some convincing ar-
"gument upon which I build my hope;
"or my belief in God and the doctrines
"of religion. I think it is St. Peter that
"lays down this rule in one of his epistles.
"you seem, my child, to have a great re-
"gard for the scriptures, and to be a good
"deal acquainted with them; and I could
"give you many reasons, for my being
"extremely glad that you are so. but
"now that we have mentioned the scrip-
"tures, pray could you not prove the point

"we

EXERCISES.

" we have been speaking of; the exiſtence
" of a God or of a deitie out of theſe?
" indeed, ſir, I have met with many noble
" and charming deſcriptions of God and
" of his works in the ſcriptures. but then
" I am told that theſe ſcriptures are the
" word of God. now before I can believe
" any thing to be the word of God, I muſt
" know that there is a God; for if there
" be no God, there can be no word of
" God; ſo that I think I muſt prove by
" ſome other arguments, that there is a
" God, and then that the ſcriptures are
" the word of God. from whence then
" would you derive your arguments? I
" think, ſir, it muſt be from what I have
" heard called the light of nature. the
" light of nature, child! why, what do
" you mean by that? I hope, ſir, I ſhall
" be able to give you ſome account of it,
" when we meet again."

LECTURE II.

Lect. II. IN our former interview upon this occasion we endeavoured to shew you, that, as there is certainly such a thing as thought, tho' it be not the object of our bodily senses, it does from thence necessarily follow, that there may be a thinking being, who is not to be discerned by any of those senses, since thought necessarily implies the existence of some thinking mind, in which it inheres, or of some thinking being, to whom it is belonging, and whose it is. and by this means we designed to obviate what may possibly be one of the first difficulties occurring to the mind of a child relating to the grand question, whether or no there be a God, who made him and the rest of the human species. and as much as we may be inclined to value ourselves upon being above such childish prejudices, yet many of riper years may not be altogether free from some such influence as this. and it is highly necessary for all to accustom themselves to such reflexions, as may tend in the most effectual manner to impress their minds

with

with a sense of a really existing deitie, and of his presence with us, notwithstanding his invisibilitie. and having thus gone through the first and lowest step in this argument, by shewing that there may be such a being, and that the supposition carries in it no impossibilitie or contradiction to any natural notion or sentiment, it is now our purpose to procede to the direct proof and demonstration, that there actually is such a being. this has been the common belief of all mankind in every age of the world, and throughout every region of it. the most uncultivated of human kind believe the existence of a God as firmly as the best philosophers; and that upon the same general ground, and from the force of the same kind of convictions; tho' they be not able to illustrate the argument by an equal copiousness and varietie of particulars. and from this universal consent of mankind some have seemed to think that a direct and formal proof of a divine being is to be deduced. but I cannot suppose that it amounts to more than this; that there must needs be some very strong and forcible, and at the same time very obvious reasons, upon which such a

belief

LECT. II. belief is founded; and which has produced
so universal a consent in reference to this particular, notwithstanding that almost infinite diversitie of opinion, which is in other instances so apparent. and indeed what reasoning can possibly be more forcible or evident, than that of the author of the epistle to the Hebrews: " every house is built by " some man, and he that built all things, " is God?" now this is the sum and substance of the argument in proof of a deitie. and in this single point it is, that all the illustrations of it arising from a particular and distinct survey of the works of nature must necessarily center. and surely this is an argument which no reasonable creature can justly plead an incapacitie for understanding. is there any child, who does not, in fact reason thus, upon seeing an house regularly built and divided into proper and convenient apartments; that there must needs have been some designing cause or agent, some thinking being like himself, tho' able to think more perfectly and wisely, that had been concerned in raising such an edifice? " and would not you, my child, " at least be ready to laugh at any other " child, and almost to call him fool or " idiot,

Universal consent.

" idiot, who should pretend to say, that
" the house had rose exactly into that re-
" gular form and all those convenient
" divisions by chance, and without any
" ones knowing any thing of it, or think-
" ing at all about it, or designing any such
" matter?" but how much more ridiculous must it be, and how easie to discern
that it is so, to imagine, that the whole
universe itself, in which there is such a
vastly more extensive and durable scene of
perfect order and regularitie, of happy contrivance and useful tendencies, should have
come into being without any designing or
conscious mind? what an amazingly useful and well-contrived fabric, for instance,
is the human body? with what regularitie
and ease do we by means of it perform the
various functions of life? eat, drink, move
either ourselves or other bodies, see, taste
and smell; and all with the greatest convenience imaginable, and in the same exact
method and order from day to day? what
a constant and beautiful appearance of the
sun throughout each revolving year? what
a stated order in the seasons of " summer
" and winter, seed-time and harvest," and
in the production of the several fruits of the
earth,

Lect. II. earth, (a) so that every child knows when to expect the return of these seasons and the appearance of these fruits? these are general hints capable of being illustrated by an infinite varietie of particulars; and many useful books there are of this sort, which young persons might to their greatest benefit imaginable be conversant with. books which, as they contain the fullest demonstration of the being and perfections of the deitie, so there cannot be the least objection made to them on account of any difficultie in

(a) Videmus quam certæ sint leges motuum cœlestium, certum numerum specierum, et propagari similia ex similibus, non promiscuè, alia ex aliis, videmus causas finales rerum: singula nascuntur ad aliquam utilitatem. est et mirabilis consensus superiorum et inferiorum corporum. motus cœlestes certas vices æstatis et hyemis ad utilitatem viventium efficiunt. quid fontium et fluminum perennitas? quid in corpore humano partium singularum distributio? quid ipsa numeri et ordinis agnitio? nonne testantur clarè hanc naturam non extitisse casu, sed ab aliqua æterna mente ortam esse? impossibile est enim hæc semper. ita fieri casu. impossibile est notitias numeri et ordinis casu aut ex materia tantum ortas esse. o cæcas hominum mentes, quæ tam perspicuis argumentis, tam expressis vestigiis divinitatis non moventur; ut melius de deo sentiant et eum revereantur.

Melanct. in Epist. ad *Rom.* c. i. p. 166, 167.

EXERCISES.

in understanding them, they being in the general scope and tenor of them the most intelligible that can be. I speak of such books as Ray on the wisdom of God in the creation, Derham's Physico-Theology, Nieuentyt's Religious Philosopher, Nature displayed, and the like. what pity it is, that it is not a stated point to put some such books as these into the hands of children, or at least some well chosen extracts from them? it would give them a great deal of immediate light and information; and would gradually and after the most pleasing manner strengthen their reasoning powers, and enlarge their intellectual and moral views. historie is generally thought to be a kind of reading that is best adapted to the capacities of children, and peculiarly proper for promoting the improvement of their minds, and of those of the younger sort. Now these books are no other than the historie of God's works in creation and providence; an historie altogether as intelligible as any other whatsoever; and at the same time infinitely greater consequences are depending upon the truth of it. by conversing intimately with such topics we shall come, not so much to know and to believe,

LECT. II. believe, as to see and feel, that there is a God. I might likewise have mentioned some good tranflation, if to be met with, of Cambray on the exiftence of God; or, if your children muft needs learn French, fome extracts out of that book might very properly be put into their hands upon this great fubject altogether as intelligible furely as his fables. and the reading of fuch books would be ftill more profitable and conducive to the improvement, ufefulnefs and comfort of after-life, if parents by their own perfonal addrefs and application would in a proper manner endevor to prepare, and as it were, to open the foil in which this precious feed is to be fown. fuppofe for inftance, as they fo often hear others speak of God, and do often themfelves make ufe of that name, you were to begin with afking them what they mean by

Deitie the name, term, or appellation of God. to this it is natural to imagine, they would of themfelves anfwer, that they meaned by

what. it the being, who made, and who preferves and who governs the world. they might not perhaps exprefs themfelves exactly in thefe terms, but this would be the purport of their anfwer, and a better could not be given.

EXERCISES.

given. in many writings, and I believe in most catechisms, all the attributes and perfections of God are enumerated, as explicatorie of the name or term itself, and as making a part of it. thus in one catechism, to the question what is God, I find the answer to be, " God is a spirit, infi-
" nite, eternal, and unchangeable in his
" being, wisdom, holiness, justice, good-
" ness, and truth." in another, the answer which I find to be given to the same question is; " God is a spirit perfectly
" holy, infinite in wisdom and knowledge,
" in power and in presence, necessary and
" eternal in his existence, and unchange-
" able in his blessedness." Now this I apprehend is throwing too many ideas at once into the mind of a child. nor is it, I presume, a thing even so proper in itself, according to the very nature of the subject treated of. for the word God is a relative term, and, if there be a creator and governor of the world, there is a God, whatever be the moral character or other attributes of that being. these are a matter of after consideration; in the mean time, the answer which would naturally occur to the mind of a child in the first place, upon be-

ing

Lect. II. ing asked what he meaned by the word God, is the best; that he understood by it the being who made and preserves the world. and it is the same in effect with that explication, idea, or notion of it that has been given by the noble author of the characteristics: " whatsoever, as he ex-
" presses it, is superior in any degree over
" the world, or rules in nature with dis-
" cernment and a mind, is what by uni-
" versal agreement men call God." the next question then proper to be put to the child is, why he believes that there is such a being. " and here, my dear child, you
" remember, that in the last conversation
" we had together upon the subject, you
" told me that the existence of a God

Light of nature.

" must be proved by the light of nature;
" and you promised to inform me what
" you meant by that expression; will you
" now make that promise good? I will
" endevor it. what then do you mean by
" the light of nature? by the light of
" nature, sir, I mean all those conclusions
" which I am led to make, or principles
" which I am induced to embrace upon
" the subject of religion by the reasoning
" of my own mind from what I see or
know

"know to exist, independently of any in- LECT. II.
"formation that is given me by the scriptures
"or the bible. the light of nature then
"you say, is all that you can reasonably
"believe in matters of religion, without
"having recourse to the bible; or it de-
"notes all the arguments and reasonings
"that you can make use of in support of
"your belief in these matters, without re-
"curring to that book. and do you think
"that by this light of nature you can
"prove the being of a God? I am ready
"to think so; and if I am not mistaken,
"the bible itself assures me that I may.
"where, I pray you, do you find any such
"declaration made? I think, sir, it is in
"St. Paul's epistle to the Romans; where
"he says, that *the invisible things of God
"are clearly seen, being understood by the things
"that are made.* by *the invisible things of
"God,* I suppose to be meaned the realitie
"of God's being or existence, even tho'
"we cannot discern him with our bodily
"eyes, and by the *things that are made,*
"the visible things of the creation or the
"works of nature. but among these things Self-pro-
"do you include yourself? yes. but why duction.
"do you think that God made you?
                                "might

Lect. II. "might not you have brought yourself
"into being? I think, sir, that must have
"been impossible: because to bring any
"thing into being is an act of power;
"and therefore I could not bring myself
"into being, because I could not perform
"any action or exert any power before I
"had a being. besides, if I had brought
"myself into being, I could certainly pre-
"vent my being sick or dying; but I know
"I cannot do that. but might not your
"parents give you your being? I think
"if they had given me my being, they
"could keep me here in this world as long
"as they pleased. but I see that other
"children die, notwithstanding all that
"their parents can do for the preser-
"vation of their lives; and I suppose that
"might have been, or yet may be so with
"respect to myself; and therefore it seems
"very evident to me, that there must be
"some other being, that has more power
"over me than my parents, and over other
"children than theirs; nay, and over my
Dependant "parents themselves, for I find that none
state. "of my fellow-creatures, whether chil-
"dren or grown up to manhood, have it
"in their power to dispose of themselves
"and

" and their affairs as they please, or to LECT. II.
" stay in this world as long as they like.
" in short, I plainly perceive that man-
" kind have not either themselves or their
" affairs at their own command here upon
" earth. from whence I think it must
" certainly follow, either that there is
" some superior being, who made and
" governs them, or else that there was no
" creation, nor is now any government
" of the world at all; but that it came
" into being, and that all things happen
" in it by chance. what do you mean by Chance.
" chance? I do not mean any real being
" or cause by it, but only the coming to
" pass of this or that without thought or
" design, and without any cause at all.
" and do you think it possible that the
" world, the sun, the moon, the stars,
" the earth, with all the productions and
" inhabitants of it, the air, and the birds
" that fly in it, the sea and the fish that
" swim there, that all these could have
" come into being without some thinking,
" intelligent, and designing cause? no,
" sir; I think it to be utterly impossible.
" why so? because, sir, as you have but
" just now been saying, I plainly perceive,

C " that

" that it requires a great deal of thought
" and contrivance, of skill and dexteritie,
" to build even a single house, nay, to fit
" up in a proper manner any one apart-
" ment in it; and I am very certain that
" without the express design, purpose, and
" agencie of some thinking being, such a
" thing could never be done. and tho' I
" have some share of understanding and
" degree of contrivance in my own mind,
" yet I am very far, I am sure, from be-
" ing capable of executing any such design.
" as then the world is so vast and wide a
" place, as it abounds with such a prodi-
" gious number of conveniencies and ac-
" commodations of all sorts both for man
" and beast; as every thing is more per-
" fectly and exactly adapted for our use
" than we ourselves could have contrived
" it; as this immensely wide, extended
" scene of things is every where full of
" order, beauty, regularitie and usefulness,
" it seems to me, that it must needs be
" infinitely more clear and evident that
" there is a maker of the world, than that
" an house must needs have a builder;
" and yet of this latter I have no manner
" of doubt. I perceive it then to be your
" notion

EXERCISES.

"notion of divine creation, that this LECT. II.
"beauteous and regular system of things
"was at first framed and brought into
"being by some intelligent and designing
"mind. but this world, you know, has
"been in being, and has had the same
"regular and orderly appearance for a
"long succession of ages; can you ac-
"count for this continuance by the ori-
"ginal act of creation? or do you think
"a continued exertion of a divine provi-
"dence, and of the same active intelli-
"gence that first gave being to it, to be
"necessarie in order to account for its
"continued sustenance and support? I Sustenta-
"think, that, if God did not continually tion.
"govern the world, it could not continue
"in its present order, notwithstanding his
"first creation of it. what reason have
"you for thinking so? because I perceive,
"that in a family, my own father's, for
"instance, things would fall into great
"confusion, if he did not exercise a con-
"tinual care and inspection over it, not-
"withstanding any wise provision that he
"might have made at first for it's order
"and good management. but I think
"that as the whole universe is so much
"more extensive than a family, and as
"it

"it must be much more dependant upon it's maker than a family upon it's head, it must necessarily follow, that as a single family cannot continue in it's due order and regularitie without a continued care and inspection exercised over it, the world could not have that regular and orderly appearance it now has, and which has from the beginning been the character, form and aspect of it, without the continued providence and government of that being who first created it; and as I cannot but believe that God made it with some design and end, and as that end cannot be answered without his continued preservation of it, there seems to me to be just the same reason for believing a providence as for the idea of creation." These two arguments, which we have thus briefly mentioned, are capable of, and highly deserving a more particular illustration. we may then, I say, certainly conclude that God governs the world, because he made it; for we must necessarily suppose that he made it with some view, and with regard to some determinate end. now whatever that was, the same view, the same reference and design must necessarily determine him to preserve

EXERCISES.

and to uphold it; otherwise that end cannot be answered. just, for example, as in the making of a watch; it is not made merely for the sake of making of it, but with a view to some farther end and use; and therefore the maker or the owner of it has a continued care and inspection over it. and as it would be absurd to think that any man should make a watch, with a design when he had finished it, to let it lie by without any such care and inspection of it as would be absolutely necessary in order to its producing any effects suitable to its original formation; it would be vastly more absurd to imagine that God should create the world without a design of governing it. because without the exertion of his power in the support, as well as in the creation of it, what can we conclude, but that it must immediately sink again into nothing? consequently we must suppose, either that he had no end at all in creating it, or else, that the end has not been answered, both which are manifest absurdities. Again, secondly, a divine providence is most certainly to be infered from the actual and present order of things; because present order does just as strongly demonstrate

LECT. II. present government, as the original order of the universe implies the original production of it by some designing mind. and of the two, there must, I think, be a greater absurditie in pretending to account for the continued regularitie and order of the world from the beginning to the present time, without the continued agencie of a designing mind, than in attempting to account for the first immediate existence of it without such a designing cause; the evidence apparently heightening in proportion to the permanency of the effect. so closely is the

Providence. doctrine of a providence connected with the notion of creation. and so extremely foolish and ridiculous was that argument which some sceptics of old seem to have made use of against a providence; that "all things continued as they were from "the beginning;" which is a demonstration that there is a providence. and it is an argument too that is continually growing upon our hands: we have the experience of our own to add to that of every preceding age; and the longer the world continues in the same regularitie and order in which it now appears, so much the stronger will be the argument arising from that regularitie and order

EXERCISES.

order in favor of a divine providence and government in the universe. we should now procede to consider the nature, qualities and properties of this divine providence and rule, and the attributes and perfections of the divine being himself, did the time allow. but we must needs refer it to the next opportunitie.

LECTURE III.

IN prosecution of the several subjects which we proposed to treat upon in this our evening exercise, we endevored at our last meeting upon the occasion, to give you a brief view and illustration of those great topics, the creation of the world and the providence of God. in respect to this latter point we observed that the realitie of a divine providence exercised over the world, was most certainly to be infered even from the creation of it. for, as creation necessarily implies some end proposed by the creating deitie, whatever we imagine that end to have been, we cannot but suppose

LECT. III. pose it to be an exactly equal motive for exercising a subsequent providence over the world as for the original production of it. we likewise observed that the same truth was most clearly to be deduced from the present actual order of the world, and that regularitie of things that has subsisted for such a long succession of years and ages. since it is altogether as absurd to imagine, that the present order of the world should be the effect of chance, or not procede from some designing mind, as that it could have been constituted at first in so regular and orderly a manner without some designing cause. these reasonings we endevored to

Watch. illustrate by the similitude of a watch. that which particularly led us to the making use of this comparison was not then specified, but we will mention it now. it is a comparison that has, as we apprehend, been sometimes applied in such a manner, as to weaken the argument in favor of a divine providence, instead of strengthening or illustrating it. it has been said, that, as a watch-maker can make a watch, so as that it shall perform it's regular movements without his future inspection or care of it, we cannot suppose, unless by imputing some
kind

kind of imperfection to the divine being, that he could not in the original production of that syftem of things which we call the world, or nature, or the univerfe, imprefs fuch laws of motion and activitie, fuch a force and energie upon its component parts, as that it fhould fo long as he pleafes, continue to anfwer the end of its creation by virtue of this originally impreffed force, without ftanding in need of his immediate agencie for the direction and government of it. but, tho' a watch-maker can make a watch that poffibly may not require any farther care or infpection of his, yet this is only upon fuppofition that fomebody elfe, the purchafer for inftance, undertake to keep it in due order. and what, I pray, would a watch or any other mechanical production be good for, that nobody was to take care of? fo that the fimilitude, inftead of proving what it is generally brought to prove, that there is no neceffitie, namely, for any immediate agencie of the deitie in the prefervation of the univerfe, but that this may be very well accounted for by the powers originally impreffed upon the feveral parts of it; rather proves the direct contrary, and fhews that a divine care and infpection

LECT. III. is altogether as needful for the support and continuation of the order and regularitie of the world, as a divine power and energie to account for the first production of it. but still it may be said, that a watch will go, for some time at least, without any one's taking care of it. why then may not the universe, the production of a divine power and energie, be supposed to continue answering the ends of it's original formation for a thousand years or any longer period in exact regularitie and order by virtue of some original impressions, without needing the immediate super-intendencie and care of it's creator? but here again I must deny the truth of the assertion, that a watch can go even for a single moment without any one's taking care of it. for the art of man exerted in any of these mechanical operations, consists not in giving new laws of motion to matter, but only in accommodating those which naturally belong to it to such and such particular uses. so that every single movement of a watch depends as much upon a divine agencie supporting and maintaining the general and natural laws of motion, as even the revolution of the planets. nay, without this divine agencie

agencie the parts of which it is compofed could not fo much as adhere to one another; but, if they did not inftantly fink into nothing, would however immediately fly afunder into an infinity of atoms. for cohefion is no effential propertie of matter. this confifts of particles infinitely divifible. thofe which compofe a piece of metal are in themfelves as diftinct and feparable, as thofe which make up a heap of fand ; and their clofer union the effect only of a divine and perpetually exerted power. in fhort, without this power you can no more account for the cohefion of the parts of matter, than you can for the motion of it. and every grain of fand is in fact a proof of a deitie. in every fuch grain there is an infinitie of particles of matter naturally divifible from one another. what then can be the caufe of their coherence and juncture, but a power conftantly impreffed upon them by fome voluntarie, defigning agent? and having thus vindicated that reprefentation of things which was laid before you in our laft difcourfe, let us now procede to what we propofed for being more directly the fubject of this. and that was as you remember, the attributes of God,

Lect. III. God, and the qualities and properties of his providence. the divine attributes have generally been divided in speaking of them into those which are natural, and those which are moral. but I have sometimes wished, that the distinction intended, and for which there is a real foundation, could have been however in some other manner expressed. for by these terms of distinction some may be led to imagine, that the moral attributes of deitie are not so essential to his being, as those which we denominate by calling them natural. whereas in truth God is altogether as essentially holy and just and merciful and good as he is powerful, wise or incorporeal. his moral attributes are as truly natural (*a*) attributes, as those which we distinguish by

Divine attributes

how

(*a*) It is very justly and accurately observed by Epiphanius, that "creation did not pro-
"cede from mere will alone in deitie, as if
"any kind of reasoning or deliberation had
"been for that purpose employed, but accord-
"ing to the *essential goodness* of his nature;"
agreeably to which all his attributes and properties are to be considered. ουκ απο βουλημαιος μονον—αλλα κατα το αυιοαγαθον—p. 959, Vol. I. and to the same purpose, *ib.* αυιοαγοθοτης εσι και αυιουσια επικοινωνουσα τοις εξ αυιε εξ ουκ οντων κτισθεισι—

by that appellation: but then they are
moral too; whereas those other are not so.
and this is the proper meaning of the
distinction. There is no moral excellencie
in being eternal or almightie or self-existent, but in being holie and good there is.
there is likewise a natural foundation for
another distinction sometimes applied to
the divine attributes; that I mean of
communicable and incommunicable. yet
we cannot properly make use of it in the
room of the former. because some of those,
which we call the natural attributes of the
deitie are communicable, as well as those,
which we so justly distinguish by the name
of moral. and God has in fact communicated some degrees of power and knowlege, the image and resemblance of his own
power and of his own knowlege. neither
yet can we substitute in room of the distinction spoken of, so as fully to answer
to the meaning of it, that of imitable and
inimitable; because some of those we call
the

κτισθεισ—so ἡ Φυσικη αγαθοτης is the character of
the divine goodness, *ap.* Basil. Vol. I. p. 499,
D. and says Mr. Baxter (Life of Faith) p. 179,
all the good which God does, he doeth it from
the *goodness* of his *nature.*

LECT. III. the natural attributes of the deitie are imitable as well as his moral perfections. thus we imitate the power of deitie, by every exertion of that power, with which we ourselves are endued. and by all our improvements in knowlege we gain a somewhat nearer, tho' still an infinitely distant, resemblance to his perfect knowlege. retaining then the former distinction, let us be careful in remembering, that when we speak of the natural and moral attributes of the deitie, there is no intention to intimate that the latter are not natural, but only that they are moral likewise. " and
" now my little children, in whom *I can
" have no greater joy than to hear of your
" walking in the truth* as you advance in
" years and to contribute any thing that
" is in my power towards your doing so;
" can you tell me, which of the divine
" attributes are to be called natural, and
" which are to be distinguished by the
" name of moral? indeed, sir, I am afraid
" I cannot. you remember, no doubt, often
" to have heard of God as being eternal
" and almightie and all-wise; and of his
" being holy and pure and just and good
" and merciful. now can you not tell me,
" which

" which of thefe are to be called his moral
" attributes, and which not, but only to
" be ftyled natural? I know, fir, you will
" not be difpleafed at my giving the beft
" account I can of this matter, even tho'
" it fhould be a very miftaken one; and
" that where I am in the wrong you will
" inform me better. I will therefore ven-
" ture, if you pleafe, to tell you what my
" thoughts are concerning it. I think
" then thofe muft be God's moral attri-
" butes, for which I love him. and why
" do you love God? I love him, becaufe
" he is good and kind and merciful in
" preferving and in taking care of me and
" of all mankind; becaufe he never wrongs
" or injures any of his creatures in the
" leaft degree whatfoever; and becaufe
" I believe him to be fo very good and
" kind, that I may depend upon it that
" nothing will ever take place in his deal-
" ings towards them but what is for their
" good. I think you have expreffed your-
" felf properly and juftly. and according
" to the account you have given, I per-
" ceive that you look upon God's good-
" nefs, and mercy, holinefs and juftice as
" being his moral attributes; for thefe
                                  " alone

LECT. III. "alone are, I dare say, the things that
"you approve of in any of your fellow-
"creatures. and you say that these are the
"qualities for which you love the deitie.
"but suppose that God had been a being
"eternal, all-wise and infinitely powerful,
"but yet had not provided for the welfare
"and good of his creatures; but had em-
"ployed his power and his wisdom in
"making them unhappy and miserable;
"just as tyrannical kings here on earth
"exercise their power and use all their
"dexteritie and skill in doing things very
"cruel and barbarous: you could not
"perhaps in that case have loved him,
"notwithstanding his being eternal and
"all-wise and infinitely powerful. indeed
"I think I could not; for then I might
"likewise love a wicked, cruel tyrant,
"that takes a pleasure in enslaving, tor-
"menting and killing mankind. it should
"seem then according to this account,
"that God's eternitie and omnipresence
"and infinite wisdom and power must be
"those which we are to call his natural
(*a*) attributes. that is what I mean, sir,
"and

(*a*) After all it is to be remembered that the
words nature, natural, and the like, must needs
be

EXERCISES.

Lect. III.

Omnipresence.

" and I shall be able I think for the future
" to recollect this distinction, and to form
" an idea of it, only by considering what
" it is for which I love the deitie. the
" omnipresence of God I think you just
" now spoke of, I do not remember that
" you mentioned it before; pray what is
" it that you mean by that expression? I
" mean by it that he is every where pre-
" sent; that there is nothing done or said,
" designed or thought of, that happens or
" comes to pass in this world of ours or
" in any part of the universe, which he
" does not immediately perceive, and is
" not most exactly acquainted with. so
" that he needs not to be informed of any
" thing by any other being, having by his
" own direct and immediate inspection and
" intuition a perfect knowlege of all things.
" O sir, there is I remember, a passage in
" the Psalms, which represents this mat-
" ter, not only better than I can represent
" it, but according to my apprehension in
" a manner far better than any in which
" I have ever found it spoken of besides.
                                " I never

be but very improperly applied to the deitie,
necessarily carrying in them as they do the idea
of derivation and production into being.

LECT. III. "I never read that passage of scripture,
"but it seems some how or another to fill
"my mind with great ideas and concep-
"tions, and to raise and elevate my un-
"derstanding. you will oblige me very
"much, my dear child, if you will re-
"peat the passage you refer to, and which
"seems by your manner of speaking of it
"very much to have affected you. it has
"indeed, sir. and I very well remember
"it is at the beginning of the hundred
"and thirty-ninth Psalm. I have been so
"much pleased with it and have read it
"over so often, that I have gotten it by
"heart. *O lord, thou hast searched me and*
"*known me. thou knowest my down-sitting*
"*and mine up-rising; thou understandest my*
"*thoughts afar off. thou compassest my path*
"*and my lying down, and art acquainted*
"*with all my ways. for there is not a word*
"*in my tongue, but lo, o lord, thou knowest it*
"*altogether. thou hast beset me behind and*
"*before, and laid thine hand upon me. such*
"*knowlege is too wonderful for me; it is*
"*high, I cannot attain unto it. whither*
"*shall I go from thy spirit? or whither*
"*shall I flee from thy presence?*" this doctrine of the divine omnipresence, tho' in
the

the idea or notion of the thing itself somewhat too mighty for the grasp or compass of our understanding, yet in the proof and certainty of it is extremely obvious. for no being can act where it is not. every exertion of power must necessarily suppose the presence of some being or another in that part of space where it is exerted. and therefore as God exercises a power over all nature, he must of necessity be actually and immediately present to every part of nature. we can indeed direct or order things to be done by another, where we are not; but then it is by substituting the *presence* of that other in the room of our own. and tho' numbers of inferior agents are no doubt employed in carrying on the affairs of divine providence, yet the *presence* of the first and supremely ruling cause in nature must be necessary in order to the support of these in being and in action, wherever it is that they act. so that the ministration of these inferior agents does no way exclude the necessity of supposing God's universal presence, in order to account for his universal providence; these very beings themselves standing in need of his providential
sup-

Lect. III. support and all-sustaining energie. "but
"to you younger ones let me once more
"address myself on this head. you have
"seen what is the just and rational account
"of God's omnipresence; his presence
"in all places, and with all men; his
"most exact and intimate acquaintance
"with all things and with all events. but
"might you not, think you, farther infer
"from it some observations and rules that
"may be useful for the regulation and go-
"vernment of your own temper and
"actions. when you are in company
"with some person of rank and figure
"in the world, are you not particularly
"careful not to be rude in your be-
"havior? suppose you were to be ad-
"mitted into the presence of the king,
"would you not be very strictly upon
"your guard not to do any thing that
"should displease or appear to carry in it
"any slighting thoughts of him or disre-
"spect to him? but God is always with
"you; and he is greater than the greatest
"of earthly kings. he is *the king of kings*
"*and lord of lords.* besides, he is infinitely
"good; or rather indeed in this moral
"excellence of character must true great-
"ness

"nefs be fuppofed alone to confift. the
"divine being is *glorious in his holinefs.*
"and with refpect to human kind the
"poet's maxim muft ever ftand confeffed;
"that where virtue is wanting nobilitie
"muft be in vain pretended to *(a).* and
"I fuppofe my dear child, that the higher
"opinion you have of the goodnefs and
"excellent character of any of your fel-
"low-creatures, fo much the more folici-
"tous you are not to fay or do any thing
"amifs in their prefence. efpecially, if
"they are not only highly good and
"virtuous in their own character, but
"have alfo been very good and kind to
"you. fhould you not then be always
"upon your guard againft offending God,
"and take the ftricteft care not to do fo?
"fince he is always prefent with you. by
"no means may you think yourfelf at
"liberty to fin, to tell a lye for inftance,
"or to take into your poffeffion any
"thing that does not belong to you,
"merely becaufe no human being can hear
"or fee you. but I obferve that in every
"anfwer, which you give me to the quef-
"tions that I propofe to you upon this
"head,

(a) ——Nobilitas fola eft atque unica virtus.

Lect. III. "head, you speak only of one God. do
"you believe that there is but one? yes,
"sir, I believe in one only living and su-
"preme God. and pray what is your
"reason for this belief? I find that with-
"out supposing the existence of one God
"I cannot give any rational account of
"the appearances of things. I cannot
"without this account for my own won-
"derful frame and constitution, nor for
"the order and regularitie, which I see in
"every thing around me. but by this
"belief I can account for these things
"without supposing that there is more
"Gods than one. to believe therefore
"that there are more than one, would be
"to believe without having any reason to
"assign for the foundation of my faith."
besides, were we to suppose two or more
self-existing natures concerned in the
creation of the universe, it should seem
to follow from that puritie, equitie and
justice, which we so naturally ascribe
to divinitie, that each would determine
not to defraud or injure any other, in
relation to the equal honors that would
on this account be owing to both or all
of them. and upon this principle we
may

may I think certainly conclude, that had there been any such pluralitie, the number of co-operating deities would have been by some natural, striking, indelible and universal signature notified to mankind. yet we see nothing in the real scene of nature but what is the reverse of this. and on all these accounts the unitie (*a*) of nature seems to be an argument fully decisive for the belief of one only creating mind. "but does not the
" scripture say, that *there are Gods many and*
" *Lords many?* yes, sir, but the same scrip-
" tures say, that there is but *one God and*
" *father of all.* and *hear, o Israel, the lord*
" *thy God is one lord,* is a passage I remem-
" ber to have read in the book of Deutero-
" nomy. why then are other beings called
" Gods? I imagine it must be on account
" of some resemblance which they bear to
" the one supreme God, either in power
" or in wisdom or in goodness of charac-
" ter. besides I remember it is said in the
" scripture, *worship him all ye Gods.* which
" seems plainly to me to imply, that there
" is one supreme God, whom all other be-
                                            " ings,

(*a*) See this particular very happily illustrated in *Nature Displayed*, Vol. III. p. 304—12.

CATECHETICAL

Lect. III. "ings that are called Gods are bound
"to worſhip and adore as being infi-
"nitely above them. your notion then
"of the unitie of God is, that there is one
"ſingle being, who is the origin and ſource
"of exiſtence to all other beings, and who
"did himſelf derive his being from none?
"that is my opinion of it."

LECTURE IV.

Lect. IV. VERY cloſely connected with that
doctrine of divine omnipreſence,
which we treated of in our laſt evening
exerciſe, is that of the divine omniſcience,
or God's knowlege of all things. "for
"this I ſuppoſe my children, you know to
"be the meaning of omniſcience. it is
"the knowlege of all things." this muſt
certainly be the reſult of the divine omnipreſence. for a being that is actually every
where by an immediate, ſpiritual preſence, muſt certainly have the moſt exact
and intimate knowlege of whatever is
paſſing or tranſacted, either in the external
world

world of nature or in the heart of man. and by thus grounding the omniscience of God upon his omnipresence, we are led into the most accurate idea or notion concerning it; at the same time that we have from hence arising the most undeniable proof and demonstration of it. of all that is passing without us, there is nothing which we ourselves know so perfectly as that, which is the object of our sight. and if we could with our bodily eye command the whole world itself, just in the same manner as we do the extent of such a place as this, most truly might we then say that the whole world was the object of our knowlege. now God in consequence of his omnipresence knows every thing as perfectly as we know any thing that is before our eyes; his knowlege of all things is not the effect of any investigation or application of mind, but of immediate intuition; in the same manner as external objects are fully subject to our visual organs without any intervening study or labor of our thoughts. thus it is that God is " not far from every one " of us." all creatures lie " naked, open " and manifest to his eye." because it is " in him that we and all creatures live and " move

LECT. IV. "move and have our being." but it is here by all means to be remembered, that the divine ubiquitie or omnipresence is alike predicable with respect to duration as to space. so that the divine nature or essence is, truely speaking, co-existent with eternity. and hence arises the true account of that which is perhaps somewhat improperly called the divine prescience or foreknowlege. that those events and transactions which are future to us, are all of them most exactly and intimately known to deity, is a thing not to be questioned. but then in order to a clear conception upon this point, it is to be carefully recollected, that tho' future to us, they are not so to deitie, but that they are to him actually present (*a*).

under

Divine fore-knowlege what.

(*a*) "Strictly speaking, says Mr. Sturmy, "*fore-knowlege* is a term which does not suit "with the perfection of the divine under- "standing; but it is a condescensive expres- "sion to our capacity; denoting God's cer- "tain, instant and punctual knowlege of many "actions and things, which are future to his "creatures. For the knowlege of creatures is "gradual; and to them the drama of provi- "dence is displayed by a broken succession of "parts; the infinite understanding is not like "a finite understanding, whose imperfect capa- "city obligeth it to divide duration into *past*, "*present*,

EXERCISES.

under this attribute too of omnipresence, will very naturally be comprehended the divine

LECT. IV.

"*present, and future.* I say it is not thus with
"the understanding of God; there is no di-
"vision in his duration; no process in his
"views; no progress in his knowlege: for
"all duration, actions, things and persons are
"equally present to the infinite mind: he sees
"not as man sees, nor knows as man knows:
"he grasps all objects with one continual
"view, distinctly without confusion and with-
"out distraction. historie and remembrance,
"prediction and event, faith, sight and sci-
"ence give us a different, nay sometimes an
"opposite representation of the same things:
"but God's ideas of all things are as one idea,
"simple and uniform, from everlasting to
"everlasting: he is the first and the last, and
"can declare the end from the beginning, and
"from ancient times the things that are not
"yet done." See his Sermons, No. IV. p. 82,
83. " all things, says Mr. Tryon, whether
"past, present, or to come, appear *present* to
"the great eye of the eternal being."—and
again, " the Lord sees and knows all things,
"for unto him there is neither *time* nor place,
"night nor day, but *all* is *essentially present*;
"for things in eternitie go not by degrees or
"by progressions as they do in time." See his
Discourse on Dreams and Visions, c. xii. p. 220,
221. To the same purpose Bishop Bramhall
in his *Castigations* of Mr. Hobbes, p. 49.
"every particular event that shall be unto the
"end

Lect. IV. divine immensitie. the omniprefence of God is his immensitie. and the immensitie of God is his omniprefence or ubiquitie. but how, it may be afked by fome of the younger clafs at leaft, can God be in all places at one and the fame inftant, or every where at once? I anfwer, it is evident that even we ourfelves may be prefent in different parts of fpace at one and the fame time. this very place for example, in which we are met, is divifible into an innumerable quantitie of diftinct portions of fpace, yet we are prefent in the whole

Immenfitie.

" end of the world is foreknown, or to fpeak
" *more properly,* is known to God from all eter-
" nitie. for in God's knowlege there is nei-
" ther before nor after, paft nor to come.
" thofe things which are paft or to come to us,
" are always prefent to God, whofe infinite
" underftanding (that is himfelf) doth encom-
" paffe all times and events in one inftant of
" eternity, and fo doth prevent or anticipate
" all differences of time. time is the meafure
" of all our acts; but God's knowlege, being
" infinite, is not meafured but by eternity; fo
" that which is a prefcience, or a *before-hand*
" knowlege (as he calleth it) to us, is a prefent
" intuition with God." Temporalia movens (fc. Deus) *temporaliter* non movetur: nec *aliter* novit facienda quam facta: nec aliter invocantes exaudit, quam *invocaturos* videt. Auguftin. de Civitat. Dei. L x. C. xii. p. 584.

whole of it,- in one part of it as well as another. what difficultie then can there be in conceiving that God may be prefent in the whole univerfe confidered as one vaft immenfitie of extenfion, in every part of it perfectly clear and open to his all pervading eye? " but, my dear child, you
" have, I doubt not, heard of God as an
" eternal being, and may remember eter-
" nitie to be afcribed to him, when his
" name is folemnly celebrated and adored
" in *the affemblies of his faints.* what, I
" pray you, may be the idea or notion that
" you form of this divine attribute? it
" means, fir, I think, that there was no
" beginning of God's being, and that
" there will never be an end of it. and
" this I fuppofe, fir, to be the reafon why
" God is faid in fcripture to be the *only*
" *being that has immortalitie*; becaufe, tho'
" there are other beings, whofe exiftence
" will never have an end; fuch as angels
" and myfelf, my own foul, and all my
" fellow-creatures of the human race, yet
" we and all the angels had a beginning of
" exiftence. but I find it to be declared
" in the fcriptures that God is from ever-
" lafting, as well as to everlafting. fo
" that

Lect. IV.

Eternitie.

LECT. IV. "that it appears to me according to the doctrine of scripture to be altogether as clear and certain, that God has been always, as that he will be for ever." all actually existing natures must either be created or uncreated, derived or underived. nothing can be plainer than this. and is it not equally plain, that all cannot be created or derived, and that consequently there must be some one being, who is underived and uncreated, and independent for it's existence upon any other, and the origin of existence to all other beings? were we to say of the being that made man, that he had derived his being from some other, the question would still remain, from whom did that other derive his existence; and so on, till we arrived in our reasoning to some first cause, or some being, who was himself derived from none. now it must be the very nature of such a being to exist, otherwise he could not exist at all; any prior cause of his existence being already excluded. but a being, whose very nature it is to exist, must needs have existed always, or from eternitie. for had he begun to exist, this could only have been by a power of existing inherent in his own nature,

Self-existence.

that

that is in other words, he muſt have exiſted before he began to exiſt. for were we to aſcribe unto him a begining of exiſtence, we muſt neceſſarily impute that begining to the exertion of ſome power which he had of bringing himſelf into being. but then this is contrary to the idea of his begining to be. becauſe to have a power of begining to be, implies ſome actually exiſting being poſſeſſed of that power. ſo that to ſuppoſe the ſelf-exiſtent being, or that being whoſe nature is to exiſt, to have had a begining of exiſtence, is a contradiction in terms. it is to aſcribe to him in the very ſame inſtant of duration, both exiſtence and non-exiſtence. and as he has thus derived his being from none, it immediately follows that his exiſtence muſt endure "to everlaſting." for there is no other being that can deprive him of his exiſtence, ſince he is not at all depending upon any other being for it. ſo that if he ceaſes to be, it muſt be in conſequence of his own eſſential nature, which yet has been ſhewn to implie being, or actual exiſtence in the very idea of it. to ſuppoſe therefore that a ſelf-exiſtent being ſhould ever ceaſe to exiſt, would be to ſup-

LECT. IV. pose existence and non-existence equally natural to one and the same being. as certain therefore as it is that God has derived his being from none, so certain is it that he can never cease to be; that is, his duration must be eternal. and upon the same principles is founded the absolute immutabilitie of his nature. as none of his attributes or perfections, all of which must necessarily enter into the very idea itself of his nature or existence, are derived from any other being, no change or alteration can possibly take place in reference to them, because that would imply some being that was the cause of such an alteration, and upon which therefore he was depending for his existence. these sentiments, which arise not so much from any medium of reasoning or chain of argument, as from a comparison of our own ideas, are most naturally and forcibly expressed in the language and style of scripture. *of old, says the Psalmist, thou, o God, hast laid the foundations of the earth. they shall perish; but thou shalt endure. yea, all of them shall wax old as a garment*; stable and permanent as they now appear to be. *but thou art the same; and thine years shall have no end.* and this

Immutabilitie.

this points out to us the meaning of that expreſſion, *I am that I am*; which is ſaid in ſcripture to be the name of God. other beings may not be in all reſpects what they now are. they are liable to any change or alteration, which the ſupreme being, who created them, may think proper to make in their nature or qualitie, circumſtances, ſituation or connexions. or he has it in his power, whenever he pleaſes, totally to annihilate and deſtroy them. but God throughout the endleſs ages of duration is one permanent and ſtably exiſting nature; that is, he always was, and ever will be the ſame he now is, without the leaſt *variableneſs or ſhadow of turning*. but what, it may be aſked, are the practical uſes to be made of ſuch reflexions as theſe? I anſwer in the firſt place, that the eternitie of God renders his moral perfections, his holineſs, juſtice, goodneſs, veracitie and mercy in the higheſt degree venerable. if we attend to the natural dictates and ſentiments of our own minds, we ſhall find that a long continuance and habit of the virtuous, that is, the godlike temper in any of our fellow-creatures, a ſeries of many years all ſpent in uſeful, honorable actions without inter-

LECT. IV. interruption or intermiſſion, greatly exalts the idea we form of any one's character. it heightens our apprehenſion of the dignitie and perfection of his virtue. upon this principle is founded that maxim of Solomon ; *the hoarie head is a crown of glorie, if it be found in the way of righteouſneſs.*

Old age.
" when it is *found* in the way of righteouſ- " neſs." not when a man begins in his old age to think of the " way of righte- " ouſneſs," but when he is *found* in it having been long purſuing it ; *found* in it as in his wonted track. and when this is the caſe, we cannot but form an higher idea of the virtue of ſuch an òne, on account of its permanencie and ſtabilitie, than of that which we diſcover in thoſe of younger years. and when we riſe in our thoughts from human virtue to that which is angelic, of this latter we ſtill form a more elevated idea, when we conſider that theſe angelic natures have for a ſo much longer period, for millions and millions of ages longer, been inured to the temper of virtue than any human creatures. but, if the caſe be ſo, how inexpreſſibly venerable and adorable muſt be the moral excellencies of that being who is " from everlaſting to " ever-

"everlasting;" who has been for endless ages past, and will to all eternitie be absolutely pure, holie, righteous, merciful and good? by confidering eternitie as applicable to all thefe moral attributes of the deitie, and purfuing the reflexion with ferioufnefs and devotion, we fhall foon perceive them difclofing themfelves to our intellectual and moral eye in far greater majeftie and grandeur, than could poffibly be the cafe without this concomitant idea. when therefore we would raife our minds to the higheft admiration of the divine holinefs, let us rememember that it is eternal holinefs; of the divine mercie, that it is everlasting mercie; of divine goodnefs, that it is immutable and ever-flowing, yet never to be exhaufted goodnefs, and if fo, what intenfe and ardent, what fixed and abiding love muft it naturally call for at our hands? if God be unchanging in his love to us, ought not we to be fo in our returns of praife and gratitude to him? thus it is that on the wing of thefe fublime and glorious truths, confidered in their mutual connexion and reference to each other, we may foar and range in the devout contemplation of our minds throughout that feemingly dark and mysterious

Lect. IV. mysterious region even of eternitie itself. and then farther in the second place in the eternitie and immutabilitie of God, of the divine nature and of the divine attributes, we have the strongest foundation for our absolute trust and confidence in deitie. and it is a belief essentially necessary in order to our placing this intire dependance upon him. "I am the lord, he has declared by "his prophet, I change not, *therefore* ye "sons of Jacob are not consumed." among our fellow-creatures we meet with great flexibilitie and change of temper. those who at one time seem to be all kindness, sweetness and love, so that you might think there was nothing too great to be expected from their generositie, are at another time, and perhaps after a very small intervening space, so rough and rugged, so severe and boisterous in their manners and behavior, that you would be apt to think on the other hand, that there was nothing which might not justly be feared from their displeasure. but how unspeakable the comfort to us the creatures of the sovereign deitie, of him, who is the "father of "lights, the author and giver of every "good and perfect gift," that his goodness
cannot

cannot for so much as a single moment be intermitted; that there cannot in any instance whatsoever of his conduct towards his creatures be the smallest deviation from it. so that it is only in consequence of this immutabilitie of the divine nature that we have to say, *God is my rock and my fortress, my high tower, my buckler and my sure defence.* again; from the eternitie of God a very natural, easie and convincing argument may be drawn in proof of the immortalitie of our own souls, and of a never-ending existence ordained for man.
" you are not to wonder, my dear chil-
" dren, if what we have hitherto been
" saying should not in all particulars ap-
" pear to you for the present so intelligible
" as you could wish. even the most ex-
" alted minds cannot fully comprehend the
" amazing glories of the divine and sove-
" reign being; and it is a subject that will
" please and employ us to all eternitie.
" *canst thou by searching find out God? canst*
" *thou find out the almightie to perfection,* are
" questions you know, that are addressed
" in scripture not to children only, but to
" men too of the most mature and ripened
" understandings; so that you are not to
" be

LECT. IV. "be discouraged by any thing which may
"be said, that at present you cannot so
"easily comprehend. but you are to *fol-*
"*low on to know the lord.* and the more
"you desire and love to know of him, the
"better will you be acquainted with him.
"*then shall ye know, if ye follow on to know*
"*the lord.* God, you have often heard it

Deitie in- "said is incomprehensible ; and a great
comprehen- "and most certain truth it is, that he is
sible. "so. and this incomprehensibilitie of the
"divine nature is usually and very justly
"enumerated among the attributes of the
"divine being. and you, my child, be-
"lieve, I doubt not, that God is incom-
"prehensible. but give me leave to ask
"you what it is that you mean when you
"ascribe to him such an attribute. you
"do not, I presume, mean by this, that
"you can know nothing at all of God?
"no, sir, but only that I cannot know
"him fully ; that I cannot now, nor in
"any farther period of my existence, know
"so much concerning God, but that still
"something more will remain to be known
"of him. you are not then you appre-
"hend on account of the incomprehensi-
"bilitie of God to despise that knowlege
"of

" of him, which you can attain to, or
" to discourage yourself from pursuing it;
" but only to learn humilitie, and to ani-
" mate yourself in this inquirie, as you
" grow up and improve in understanding,
" and to increase your admiration of the
" divine excellencies thus appearing too
" bright, too illustrious, too perfect for you
" to form a full and adequate idea of them.
" I thank you, sir, for having expressed
" my own meaning and apprehension in
" this matter. but, my dear child, tho'
" perhaps that particular topic we have
" been speaking of, the eternitie of God,
" may seem to be as much as any beyond
" our comprehension; yet possibly by at-
" tending a little to it, you may perceive
" that it gives you great encouragement to
" think, that your own and the souls of
" your fellow-creatures of mankind will
" survive this present state of being, and
" are immortal. for let me ask for what
" end was it, do you imagine, that God
" at first brought you into being? indeed,
" sir, I cannot conceive for what reason it
" could be, unless it was that he might
" make me happy. for I cannot by any
" of my actions, or by any of the devotions
" that

Lect. IV. "that I pay to him, be *profitable unto him,*
"*as he that is wife is profitable unto himself,*
" according to what I remember to have
" met with in the book of Job. you seem
" then to think that God is in his own
Divine feli- " nature a perfectly happy being. indeed,
citie.
" fir, this is what I have always thought
" concerning the deitie, fince I have been
" able to think at all upon his great and
" awful nature. and pray what have been
" your reafons for entertaining a fentiment
" of this kind ? I imagine, fir, that as all
" other beings are under the controle and
" government of the deitie, it muft needs
" be impoffible that any fhould have it in
" his power to difturb his felicitie. I think
" that as he has in himfelf a fullnefs of
" being, as he is himfelf the fource and
" origin of all other beings or exifting
" natures whatfoever, he either cannot
" want any thing to make him happy, or,
" if he could, has power in himfelf to
" produce it immediately. he that can
" make all other beings happy, muft needs
" be himfelf infinitely happy. you fup-
" pofe then that God could have no other
" defign in creating you than to make you
" happy ? and for the fame reafon, I pre-
" fume,

"   fume, no other defign in making any
"   other beings like yourfelf, than that
"   they too might be happy? that is my
"   opinion. but you have learned, that as
"   God did at firſt make you, ſo he conti-
"   nually preferves you. and why do you
"   think he exerciſes all-this care for your
"   prefervation? I think it muſt be for the
"   fame reaſon for which he made me; that
"   is, out of love. well then, if God cre-
"   ated you in order to make you happy,
"   and preferves you in being for the ſame
"   end; and is, as you have juſt been told,
"   eternal and unchangeable in all the per-
"   fections of his nature, you cannot but
"   fuppoſe that he will continue to all
"   eternitie to have the fame intention in
"   reference to your happineſs. I cannot
"   but apprehend ſo; becauſe if he ſhould
"   not, there muſt then, I think, be ſome
"   change or alteration in his nature."

LECTURE V.

Lect. V. IN the service of the last Monday evening we treated more distinctly of the divine eternitie, incomprehensibilitie and happiness. whether there be a God or not, we cannot but have the idea of an eternal duration both past and to come. but what a joyful and triumphant reflexion is it to think that this eternal duration has been, and will be occupied and possessed by an eternal deitie of infinite goodness, wisdom and power! and on the other hand, what a chilling imagination would it be, and how confounding to all the powers of the soul, to think that in this eternal duration there never had been, and consequently never can be, any such supremely designing, intelligent and gracious mind. for if this world and all the beings that inhabit it, might at first have come into existence by chance, as is by the atheist supposed, it may likewise continue by chance, and it may chance too that thro' all eternitie there may be such rational conscious beings as mankind, and yet no gracious

EXERCISES.

cious father or friend to be their guide and guardian. who could suppose only such an eternal state of things, or rather such eternal confusion and anarchie, without the utmost horror and distress of soul! but our prospect into futuritie, thanks to heaven, is quite the reverse. this we have endevored distinctly to shew in our last discourse, and the sum of our argument was as follows. as every thing that has a begining must have a cause, it seems to be equally evident that what has no cause can have no begining. and to suppose that a being whose essential nature it is to exist, should ever have began to exist, is in realitie to suppose him at once existing and non-existing; since that begining could be owing to no other cause than to the exertion of a power inherent in this very being itself to bring itself into existence. but this is to suppose it to have existed before it began to exist. the more we reflect upon it, the more clearly shall we perceive that an uncaused being must have been an eternal one, and consequently must continue existing throughout an eternitie of duration. since there is no superior being, who can have any power over an uncaused and essentially

exist-

Lect. V. existing nature, so as to make the least alteration even in the manner of it's existence, much less to destroy it. we shewed in particular of what great use, and of how pleasing a nature were these considerations of God's eternitie, when applied to the moral perfections and attributes of his nature. and we might have added that it is a consideration that should prodigiously heighten our gratitude for the privileges of our own being; for, tho' bestowed in time, yet have they been the matter of eternal counsels. and upon the foregoing principles in relation to the eternitie and immutabilitie of the divine nature, it must needs be evident that God has from all eternitie had thoughts of love and kindness and mercy towards us. a reflexion that gives a kind of infinite value to every blessing we enjoy. but it is likewise equally true of the divine power and wisdom, which are the subjects now to be considered, as of the moral attributes of the deitie, that they are eternal. and it is only by considering the eternitie of all these attributes in conjunction, that our joy and triumph in God can be completed. were he eternally benevolent, but not eternally powerful and wise,

wife, in that case his benevolence would be equally lovely and adorable, yet we could not, it is evident, have the same dependence upon it as now we may, for want of an equally extended and durable power and corresponding wisdom, by which it might execute it's gracious purposes. but, when we reflect that it is one and the same being that is eternally benevolent, eternally wise and powerful, there is then nothing wanting to render our joy and confidence in God secure and complete. and with these convictions deeply possessing our minds, we may procede with full satisfaction and inexpressible delight to the more distinct consideration and survey of these several attributes themselves. first then, in relation to the wisdom of God. " I need not, I sup-
" pose, my dear children, inform you what
" wisdom is. I doubt not but you have
" often reflected with no small pleasure
" upon your own. now, if you will only
" begin with that idea, which is so fami-
" liar to your minds, and carry on your
" thoughts upon the subject, you will
" soon come to form a prodigiously high
" and exalted notion of the wisdom of
" God ; and at the same time will perceive
" that

Wisdom.

Lect. V. "that there is the greatest reason in truth
"and nature for your doing so. thus for
"example, when you have carried the
"idea of your own wisdom as far as you
"can for shame, you will, I doubt not,
"be ready to acknowlege that God is a
"great deal wiser than you. I should not
"only think myself very prophane and arro-
"gant, but also very foolish, if I did not.
"because, whatever wisdom I have, or were
"it ten thousand times more than it is, I
"must have received it from God, and am
"intirely indebted to him for it. and he
"that gave me all the wisdom I have, must
"needs be himself wiser than I. then,
"for the same reason, my dear child, God
"must be wiser than the wisest man upon
"earth; because, whoever that man may
"be, he has, as truly as yourself, received
"all the wisdom he possesses, from the
"same God, to whom you are indebted
"for yours. and were you to add to the
"wisdom of the wisest amongst men that
"of another who may be supposed to come
"the nearest to him in the share he en-
"joys of this qualitie, still the wisdom
"of God must for the same reason be
"greater than the wisdom of these two
"men

" men put together. (could we indeed
" confider thefe refpective qualities as be-
" ing diftinct aggregates, and were not
" rather led to look upon the wifdom of
" the one as being virtually comprehended
" in that of the other.) all of it, that is
" by either of them poffeffed being no
" other than a derivation or communica-
" tion from him. upon the fame princi-
" ple the wifdom of God muft needs fur-
" pafs all the wifdom of all the men that
" have ever lived in the world, or that
" ever will live in it, of all that ever have
" or ever will inhabit any other planet,
" nay, and of all the angels of heaven,
" were the wifdom of all this immenfe
" number of beings put together, fo as to
" form the accumulated endowment of
" one mind or confcious being, becaufe
" all this wifdom has been in realitie de-
" rived from God. and it cannot be, but
" that he muft himfelf have more wifdom
" than what in this kind he has communi-
" cated to any of his creatures, or to all
" of them in conjunction. by attend-
" ing a little to fuch reflexions as thefe,
" you will be led to form a very high and
" elevated idea of the divine wifdom, and

" yet

LECT. V. "yet an idea that is capable of being pro-
"digiously increased by other reflexions
"upon the same subject. thus, for in-
"stance, you told me in the last confe-
"rence we held, that God, you thought,
"made you with a design that you should
"be happy. but wisdom consists in pro-
"secuting this or that design, which any
"conscious and thinking being has in
"view after such a manner as is best adapt-
"ed for accomplishing such an end. now,
"the more diligently you attend to the
"frame of your own mind, the more evi-
"dently you will perceive how exactly
"the various powers and affections be-
"longing to it, are in the nature and
"tendencie of them fited for the promoting
"and advancing of your happiness. wis-
"dom, or the capacitie for it, reason, is
"far from being the only qualitie or en-
"dowment belonging to your soul or
"thinking part; of this I doubt not your-
"self are very sensible. you have a love
"of knowlege, a desire of being ac-
"quainted with persons, things and oc-
"currences, and of being informed con-
"cerning this or that. this is a natural
Curiositie. "curiositie belonging to your minds,
"which,

EXERCISES.

"which, tho' now it may be exercifed Lect. v.
"only in comparatively fmall and trifling
"matters, yet as you advance in years, if
"you advance in wifdom and goodnefs
"alfo, as I hope will be the cafe, will
"put you upon many inquiries of the
"higheft moment, and will be the means
"of affording you a prodigious deal of
"fatisfaction and delight. and how great
"muft be the fum of pleafure arifing from
"fuch a curiofitie or love of knowlege and
"defire of improving it, as concomitant
"with your eternal exiftence! befides you
"have a natural inclination to love virtue, Virtue.
"as you will eafily perceive by confider-
"ing only why it is that you love one
"perfon better than another. you will
"always find it to be on account of fome
"virtuous qualities, fome good temper and
"difpofition of mind, of which you fup-
"pofe fuch an one to have a larger fhare
"than another, or in whom at leaft fuch
"qualities are to you more apparent. you
"have likewife a natural principle of grati-
"tude belonging to you, of which you will
"be very fenfible if you confider only how
"prodigioufly you are fhocked and have
"your indignation excited, and how you

"are

"are even struck into amazement, when
"you hear of any ill returns that have
"been made by one man to another, who
"has bestowed a great many favors upon
"him; and of mens using those very
"basely and ill, by whom they themselves
"have been treated with the greatest kind-
"ness and good-will. now this is a prin-
"ciple of great use in societie, and to you
"as a member of it. for you are to recol-
"lect that all mankind are endued with the
"same principles of nature as yourself; so
"that whatsoever you find to be a natural
"principle of your own mind, you may
"conclude to be in like manner belonging
"to every other human being. for God
"has *fashioned the hearts of all men alike*;
"as you know the scripture expresses it in
"the thirty-third Psalm. this principle
"of gratitude is likewise a natural foun-
"dation for religion, and for the worship
"and devout admiration of God, to whom
"we are under infinite obligations; who
"is our constant and unwearied bene-
"factor, and whom therefore, gratitude
"alone, according to it's genuine ten-
"dencie and influence, could not but
"dispose us to serve and honor, to love
"and

"and obey (a). I suppose likewise, you
"will find yourself to be naturally endued
"with the desire of a future existence,
"with a fondness for your own being, and
"for the continuation of it in some future
"state, and that this even excites in your
"breast a strong apprehension and expec-
"tation that it really will be continued;
"even tho' after a while you must cease
"to be an inhabitant of the world you
"live in now. for if you had the least
"apprehension of ceasing to be, ask your
"own mind whether it would not be con-
"ceived of by you as a fate most deplora-
"ble and dreadful, and of all things to be
"deprecated and abhorred. now this de-
"fire and love of immortalitie and expec-
"tation of it, is not only very pleasing
"and

marginalia: Lect. V. Future existence.

(a) Etenim, judices, cum omnibus virtuti-
bus me affectum esse cupiam, tamen nihil est
quod malim, quam me et gratum esse et videri.
hæc est enim una virtus, non solum maxima, sed
etiam mater virtutum omnium reliquarum. quid
est pietas, nisi voluntas grata in parentes? qui
sunt boni cives? qui belli, qui domi de patria
bene merentes, nisi qui patriæ beneficia me-
minerunt? qui sancti, qui religionem colentes,
nisi qui meritam diis immortalibus gratiam
justis honoribus & memori mente persolvunt?
Cicer. pro *Planc.*

LECT. V.

"and delightful to you at present, it not only gives you a very high sense of the dignitie and excellence of your nature, but also tends to inspire you with the desire of being happy in another world, and consequently of pleasing God at present, in order to that end. on all these accounts then must you not immediately perceive that both your own and the common nature of mankind is most advantageously and suitably formed for the pursuit and attainment of that happiness, which you suppose to have been the design and purpose of God in making you and the rest of your fellow-creatures. and if this be the case, then have you, my dear child, in the frame and constitution of your own mind, and consequently in the general fabric and

Human nature.

constitution of human nature throughout all the species, a farther proof of the divine wisdom to be added to the former one in order to strengthen, enlarge and heighten your notion of this divine attribute. God designed you for happiness. he has most admirably fited the powers and affections of your nature for the attainment of it. you cannot
"there-

" therefore but afcribe wifdom to your LECT. V.
" creator. but of this you may be ftill
" farther and more effectually convinced
" by confidering in conjunction with what
" has been already laid before you upon
" this fubject, the ftate and order of the
" material world. matter has not in itfelf Material
" any wifdom or thought. it is quite an world.
" unmeaning, infenfible thing. the fun
" itfelf has no confcioufnefs of it's own
" luftre and ufefulnefs; and is altogether
" as incapable of a fentiment or a thought
" as is a clod of earth. there is not any
" part of your own body that would fo
" much as have any feeling, fo far is it
" from having any wifdom, were it not for
" the fpirit, foul, or mind that animates
" it. and therefore it is, that when this
" foul or fpirit is retired and withdrawn
" from it, the body becomes at that very
" inftant motionlefs and infenfible, even
" tho' all the limbs and organs be as yet
" remaining in the fame form, contexture
" and pofition as before. but, tho' mat-
" ter be in itfelf wholly infenfible and
" deftitute of all thought and wifdom, yet
" in the order and arrangement of its parts,
" and in the ftructure and formation of

E 3 " thofe

LECT. V. "those several bodies which compose and
"constitute the external world or visible
"scene of nature are the highest possible
"marks of wisdom and design. thus for
"example, our own bodies in particular
"are most wonderfully made and contrived
"for usefulness. with what ease and rea-
"diness, my dear child, do you move from
"one place to another? what a great va-
"rietie of objects can you command with
"your eyes, without being put to the
"least trouble or fatigue in order to your
"seeing of them? with what readiness do
"you both see and hear, and feel and taste,
"and smell and converse with your friends,
"all at one and the same time; and all
"the while your blood is circulating, the
"digestion of your food is going on, and
"every part of your body is receiving
"nourishment and strength, and you your-
"selves growing up apace into men and
"women. think you not that there must
"have been a great deal of wisdom and
"art and counsel in order to these effects?
"did you ever hear of or see any in-
"strument or machine, that performed so
"many different motions and operations
"at once, and with so much readiness and
                                    "ease?

EXERCISES.

" eafe? do you think there is any man
" upon earth that can form any ſtructure
" that for beautie and commodiouſneſs
" ſhall be comparable to an human bodie?
" whoſe contrivance is it then? it is not
" yours. it is not that of any human be-
" ing. it is not, according to what has
" juſt now been intimated, any art or ſkill
" belonging to inanimate nature itſelf,
" or to the clay that your bodies are made
" of. ſo again; if the ſun, that vaſt and
" ſplendid luminarie, had been in any other
" poſition than what it is with reſpect to
" our earth, either you and all the world
" would have been ſet on fire, or elſe you
" muſt have been frozen to death. how
" comes it then to paſs, that for ſo many
" thouſand years together, day after day,
" it ſhould ſo continually obſerve that ex-
" act regularitie and perfect order in its
" appearance, to which we are indebted
" under God for every bleſſing of our ani-
" mal life and being? that it ſhould with
" ſo much conſtancie and perſeverance
" nouriſh the earth, cauſe the corn and
" the graſs to grow for the refreſhment of
" man and beaſt, beautifie the flowers of
" the field and *bleſs the ſpringing thereof,*
" invi-

T. V. " invigorate our own bodies, and supply us
" in a regular succession of hours with its
" enlightening beams both for our pleasure
" and for our accommodation and conve-
" nience in carrying on whatever transac-
" tions we may be engaged in ? how comes
" it to pass, that not so much as for one
" day, no, not for one hour, it should ever
" disappoint our dependance upon it; but
" that without the least failure his *going*
" *forth should be from the end of the heaven,*
" *and his circuit to the ends of it* ; *and that no-*
" *thing should be hid from the heat thereof?* upon
" the earth what a regular production of the
" same kind of vegetables and fruits fited
" for the use and benefit of man ? all ap-
" pearing in the same order, in the same
" shape, form and season from year to year
" continually ? all the same species of
" brute animals feeding upon, and nou-
" rished by these fruits of the earth ? the
" bodies of these all of them exquisitely
" formed, and yet in the greatest varietie
" of kinds ? the air and the sea continu-
" ally stocked with the same sort of inha-
" bitants, all of them perfect, according
" to their respective natures ; and exactly
" fited to enjoy themselves in the elements
" to

"to which they are respectively belong-
"ing? do you think it possible that there
"should be such a constant, regular suc-
"cession and order in these things, were
"there not some wise contrivance by
"which it is effected, and to which it is
"owing? if you see the same sort of busi-
"ness or affairs carried on in any familie,
"in that for instance of which any of you
"may be a branch, or in any other; one
"thing regularly done after another, one
"person having this employment, and an-
"other that, regularly belonging to him,
"and going about it from day to day with-
"out variation, you are very sure that all
"this does not happen by chance, but that
"there is some design, some meaning and
"intention in it; and some wise man or
"woman, one or more, that conduct these
"affairs, and order them to be as they are.
"but is there not a vast deal more of or-
"der and regularitie in the operations of
"nature than in any merely human schemes
"or contrivances? the order of the best
"regulated familie is no better than con-
"fusion, when compared with the order of
"the world itself. surely then there must
"be some wise, intelligent being, that super-
"intends

LECT. V.
"intends and guides the affairs of it. or,
"let me afk you, in order to a fomewhat
"different illuftration of this matter, whe-
"ther you do not think it a piece of very
"exquifite fkill, for any one to draw with
"a lively, piercing likenefs the picture of
"a human bodie, or of any brute animal?
"or to exhibit in painting a reprefentation
"of the firmament or of the fea, or of any
"particular fcene in nature? furely you
"efteem it fo. muft it not then, I would
"afk you, implie far greater fkill to have
"brought into being the very things them-
"felves? and if you admire the art of a

Pictures.
"man who can draw a few pictures, how
"great muft be the wifdom of that being,
"who contrived the whole plan of the uni-
"verfe! for all the wifdom that is now
"apparent in the beautie and order of pro-
"vidence muft needs originally and effen-
"tially have refided in the mind that go-
"verns all. what an amazing idea then
"muft it give you of the divine wifdom,
"that it excedes the wifdom of all rational
"natures put together, with all that is
"apparent in the exquifite fymmetrie and
"contrivance of the corporeal fyftem;
"for that mind which alone produced
"thefe,

" these, must needs be superior in wisdom
" to all that these discover or possess. and
" from such a view of the wisdom of
" deitie, you cannot but collect, that it is
" so perfect, as that there must be an utter
" impossibilitie of it's being baffled, or
" in any of it's measures defeated by a
" superior skill. since there is no wisdom
" by any other being throughout universal
" nature possessed of which he is not him-
" self the giver. it is farther evident
" from this view of it, that as the mea-
" sures of divine wisdom cannot be frus-
" trated or defeated by any opposing mea-
" sures, it must needs likewise be in itself
" sufficient for directing the events of the
" whole universe in a manner completely
" answerable to the final ends and purposes
" of a divine government in nature; the
" whole universe being no other than the
" product and contrivance of that wisdom
" itself, which therefore it must needs be
" able with an infallible certaintie through-
" out all the parts of it to manage and
" direct. so that whatever be the designs
" and purposes of divine and heavenly
" love, nothing can possibly hinder the
" accomplishment of them by that wisdom
" which

Lect. V. "which is also divine." such then are the evident and undeniable proofs of a perfect, absolute and unerring wisdom essentially belonging to the supreme, eternal mind. and after what has now been offered upon this topic, we need not perhaps be very particular in insisting upon that other attribute of power, as alike belonging to the sovereign nature. the manner of proving it, and even the proofs or evidences themselves being in effect the very same with the proofs that have been adduced of the divine wisdom, and the manner in which we have endevored to illustrate them. that which is wisdom in the contrivance being just so much power in the execution. and it being by the exertion of power only that the proofs of wisdom become apparent, just so many as we have of the divine wisdom, so many of necessitie must there be occuring likewise of the divine power. so again, according to the purport and tenor of the preceding argument, the power of God must needs be greater than all human power, the power of the inhabitants of all the planets, the power of all the angels and arch-angels, greater, I say, than the power of all these

Power.

col-

collected, if it were possible, so as to constitute in a proportionable amount, the force or power of some one single and individual being; because all this power is originally and alone derived from him. all which therefore in this united view of it, the divine power must needs excede. it is therefore a power not to be controled by any. whatever may be the malice of infernal agents, and how great soever may be their power, when compared with some other created beings, yet have they no more power against God than a worm of the earth. " he ruleth for ever by his might, and all nations," the inhabitants of every world, " are but as the small dust " of the balance before him."

LECT-

LECTURE VI.

Lect. VI.

WE have now gone through the illustration of those which are called the natural attributes of the deitie, by way of distinction from such as are moral. some account of which distinction has likewise been laid before you. the sources of proof and argument upon these several topics have been pointed out; and from what has been delivered in relation to them, many very interesting particulars may be collected in reference to the attributes and character, the qualities and properties of Providence his providence; another topic, which we at first mentioned as designed to be insisted upon in this our evening exercise. rather indeed, the proof upon these several subjects is one and the same. thus for instance, it has been proved that God is a powerful and almightie being. and from hence, or rather from the proof that has been given of it, we cannot but conclude that his providence must be a powerful providence; power, as an attribute of his nature, being proved from the real appearances of actual

power

power in the productions of the visible
creation, and in the regular course and
stated order of the world. so again we
have shewn that the power of God must
needs be in the nature of it absolutely un-
controlable and irresistible. from hence it
follows that this must needs be a qualitie
belonging to all the actual exertions of it.
a being that is in his nature above all controle, must needs be so in his operations
too. men are oftentimes forced to exert
even their own power in doing things,
which they had rather not do, being controled by the superior power of others in
this or that particular project or pursuit.
in these cases, which very often happen,
they do, as we express the matter, as well
as they can ; but God always does what he
will. and from what we have been saying
likewise concerning his wisdom, as being
an essential attribute of his nature, it must
needs appear that in all the actual measures
of his providence he procedes in the manner that is most exactly and completely
adapted for the accomplishment of those
designs and purposes, which he originally
had in view, and which depend upon those
moral attributes which yet remain to be
con-

(margin: LECT. VI. its characters)

LECT. VI. considered. but whatever may be these ends, it appears from what has been already said, that they cannot but be wisely pursued ; for God is a wise being, absolutely and infinitely wise. now a wise being, " you my children will easily perceive," cannot deliberately act an absurd or a foolish part. and with respect to the sovereign mind, it is absolutely impossible that he should be induced by the force of temptation, as men often are, to act contrary to the dictates of his own wisdom and discernment. for temptations arise intirely from our own particular situation as creatures; and therefore cannot be supposed to have any existence at all with respect to the supreme and infinite creator. if God therefore be a wise being, all his productions, works, operations and measures must needs have the character of wisdom impressed upon them. besides, in the very proof which has been given of his wisdom, as an attribute essentially belonging to his nature, we have in the same manner as was observed in relation to his power, a proof likewise of the wisdom of his providence, this proof being indeed no other than the signature, the expression, the most lively striking ftriking appearance of wifdom in the conduct of that very providence itfelf. men are fometimes poffeffed of a wifdom which thro' inactivitie and indolence they fuffer to be in a great meafure conceled from the view of others. but the wifdom of God is an actually exerted wifdom. a wifdom that is perpetually manifefting and difplaying itfelf in the wonders of his providence, and in the admirable beautie, fymmetrie and order of all his works, to his intelligent and rational creatures. from the immutabilitie likewife of the divine being, another of thofe we call the natural attributes of the deitie, it neceffarily follows that all the properties as well as the defigns of his providence muft be ever uniform and the fame. as no change can poffibly be made in the power or in the wifdom of God, which are effentially belonging to his nature, his providence it directly follows muft always be a wife and a powerful providence. and as the fame marks of power and wifdom are apparent in every part of nature, from hence we collect another propertie or character of the divine providence; namely, that it is univerfal. fince thefe appearances of power and wifdom

can

Lect. VI. can only be owing to the actual, present exertion by deitie of his inherent, essential power and wisdom, which is the very thing we mean by a providence; that which the term is intended to signifie and denote. but now if God be thus irresistibly powerful and infinitely wise; if there be no being in the universe that can either controle his actions or defeat his purposes; if this power and wisdom are equally capable of being exerted in every part of the immense system of nature and over all rational agents whatsoever; and if such power and wisdom will remain essentially belonging to the deitie throughout all the endless ages of eternitie, what can be of more importance or consequence to man than the consideration of

Transition his moral attributes, which alone must determine and direct the operations of this power and wisdom? " could you, my
" child, think of any thing that would
" appear more dreadful, than that there
" should be an almightie and all-wife be-
" ing that presided over the world, who
" yet was wholly destitute of goodness;
" that had no love, no compassion, no
" forgiveness? would it not be inexpres-
" sibly terrible to you, to think that you
                            " yourself,

" yourself, that all your friends, your
" neighbors, your acquaintance, your
" kindred, the whole world itself and
" other worlds, worlds beyond worlds in
" infinite varietie, as it has been expressed,
" were all in the hands and absolutely at
" the disposal of a being thus destitute of
" mercie and of love? would not your blood
" be almost chilled in your veins, should you
" hear of a father, who is continually ex-
" ercising the utmost crueltie and inhuma-
" nitie towards his own children, exacting
" from them the most rigorous services,
" and denying them the necessarie suste-
" nance of nature, needlessly exposing
" them to all manner of danger, and suf-
" fering them to undergoe all manner of
" losses, injuries and hardships, without
" the least concern or thought of prevent-
" ing it? or when you hear of a tyrant,
" that employs all his power and abilities
" in nothing else but in acts of oppression,
" mischief and crueltie, do you not abhor
" him? and do you not shudder at the
" thought that any such man or being
" should be existing? but would it not,
" think you, be infinitely more dreadful
" and lamentable, were this the character
" of

LECT. VI.

to the moral attributes.

"of the sovereign mind? what could you then hope for at his hands? or what, on the contrary, might you not justly dread from such an ungracious being, armed with omnipotence? when some monster of a tyrant rages in the world, you know he is liable to death; he may very soon be cut off, or at most his reign cannot be very long, and after a while the world is for ever freed from so dreadful and enormous a plague. but if God were an implacable or a cruel being, he would remain so to all eternitie, and throughout every period of duration. by all your entreaties and prayers you could not in any one instance prevail upon him to be otherwise." such would be the dreadful state and condition of the world, if the God who governs and presides over it were of an evil and malignant nature. "and I have endevored, my dear children, to heighten your apprehension upon the supposition of such a government in the universe, not for the sake of terrifying you, but only with a view of rendering the contrarie persuasion so much the more delightful and welcome to your hearts. when you hear of any child that

" that has a cruel and hard-hearted father,
" such an one as we have just now been
" speaking of, does not this make you the
" more thankful that yours is of a different
" temper, gentle, mild and gracious?
" when you hear of subjects, of whole
" realms and nations, that are oppressed
" by the arbitrarie and tyrannic prince,
" does not this make you so much the
" more thankful for the freedom and hap-
" pinefs enjoyed among ourselves? in like
" manner as you could not but have the
" most terrible apprehensions concerning
" the fate of the world, of an universe, that
" was governed by an almightie and all-
" wife, but yet malignant being; this is
" a consideration, that should heighten in
" proportion the joy, the praise, the grati-
" tude of your hearts, when you consider
" and have it proved to you that the case
" is indeed directly the reverse; and that
" the great governor of the world, your
" God and my God, and the God of
" all mankind, and of all the angels and
" arch-angels of heaven, is a being as
" merciful as he is wise, as kind as he is
" mightie. for when you know that he is
" thus good, you are sure, according to
" what

"what has already been laid before you, that he will be eternally so, and can never in any inftance whatfoever or in the leaft degree deviate from this character. you will likewife be fatisfied from what has been faid concerning his power and wifdom, that as fuch a being muft necef- farily in all the meafures of his provi- dence and government have fome gra- cious intention in view, fo he will always be able to put it in execution. fo that when once you come to be firmly perfuaded and fatisfied of this divine and fovereign benevolence, you will have every thing to hope for, nothing to fear, and the ftrongeft ground for a conftant chearfulnefs and content." for thefe reafons how much fhould it be the matter of delight to us all, that the proofs of the divine goodnefs and benignitie are fo abundantly ftrong and convincing, as upon a due confideration of them cannot but be apparent. indeed they are altoge- ther as clear and as numerous, as thofe which we have of the divine power and wifdom. in the fame appearances or phæ- nomena of nature all thefe attributes are equally evident; goodnefs in the end, wifdom wisdom in the means, and power in the execution. indeed, with respect to wisdom, it is even absolutely impossible that we should be able to discover any marks or traces of it in the works of God, did we not plainly perceive some end to be aimed at in those works, because wisdom is relative to an end, and is to be judged of by it. it may be equally apparent in the prosecution of very different ends. thus a torturing engine may be made with equal wisdom and contrivance, and as much skill and dexteritie may be displayed in the formation of it, as in any piece of mechanism designed to answer the most benevolent and useful purposes. but it is evident that some end or another, either a kind or a mischievous one, or else a merely private and personal aim, must needs discover itself to our view, ere we can perceive the wisdom of this or that particular agent. and equal wisdom may appear in the prosecution, not only of different, but of directly contrary ends. thus, if the supreme being had been as malevolent, as he is kind and gracious, we should have had equal proofs of his wisdom with what we have at present. but then it would have appeared, not

in

LECT. VI. in the production of happiness, but of miserie; and the whole universe would
Inquisition. have been a kind of inquisition filled with the engines, instruments and signs of miserie; and every part of it accurately and with all possible skill and dexteritie contrived for mischief. but now on the contrarie, wherever we discover wisdom in the works of God, it is by their apparent tendencie to produce good, and to answer some kind and friendly end; to accommodate and make his creatures happy. the more his works are known, the more this appears to be the ultimate design and view of them. not one single instance in nature is there that comes within the compass of human observation, which does not thus display and manifest the goodness of its author. a few specimens more particularly and distinctly illustrated, will tend to clear and ascertain this truth. and indeed we cannot upon considering such specimens, and recollecting that the very same exactness, beautie, kind and friendly design is in every part of nature's works observable, but entertain the highest idea of that goodness. and in such specimens we shall likewise have a farther illustration of some

pre-

preceding topics; the power, for instance, and the wisdom of God. for as these attributes are essentially united in the divine nature with goodness, so the evidence of them is inseparable from the proof of it. in so close and compact a manner are these interesting truths discovered to us " by the " things that are seen;" and which so clearly demonstrate an " eternal power and " godhead." suppose then we take for our example the human eye, that so eminently useful part of our own bodily frame. in the external part of it what admirable and kind contrivance is apparent? such as these are things too generally overlooked, because they are common; but there is not the less of wisdom in them on this account; and yet vastly more of goodness, which therefore should recommend such reflexions to our attention. by the prominence of the nose the eye is very happily guarded from any external danger or injurie, which might otherways very often happen by means of a blow or a fall. the same end is likewise answered by that arch, which is erected over it. and by this arch and those coverings of it which form the brows, another very important end is served. by this means

F the

Lect. VI. the rays of light are prevented from darting so strongly and directly upon the eye, as instead of enabling us to see the better, would soon make us stark blind. of this any one may be convinced only by lifting up his head aloft and looking stedfastly at the sun. we soon find the inconvenience. and why, but because by such a posture this use of the arch of the eye is wholly prevented and set aside. and had it not been for this, to so dreadful an inconvenience we should have been continually subject, till after a while we should have been reduced to absolute blindness. by this arch likewise and its covering, as well as by the eye-lids, the sweat of the head and forehead are prevented from falling into the eye, which might otherways have proved extremely detrimental to it. the eye-lashes answer a very important purpose with respect to the safety and securitie of the eye; as by means of them the little flying particles of rubbish are prevented from falling into it. the inner part of the eye consists of various coats and humors, all regularly placed one under another; and had these been placed in any other order than that in which they really lie, the ends of vision must

EXERCISES.

must have been wholly frustrated. must there not then be a perpetual goodness, power and wisdom exerted in the regular continuation of this exact order throughout the whole species? even the very pain we feel upon the falling into the eye of some loose and wandering particle which arises from the exquisite sensibilitie naturally belonging to one of the coats of it, answers a most admirably useful and benevolent purpose; for by this means the tears are drawn out, and the thing offending washed away, which, were it long to remain, would prove not only extremely painful, but likewise a great obstruction to the sight, if not in time totally destroy it. among the several humors of the eye there is one, which is called the aqueous; of which from its nature and situation the eye may by accident happen to be deprived. but observe the benignitie of nature; there is a provision in any such case for a supplie of it. Mr. Ray, in his Treatise upon the wisdom of God in the creation, tells us of an experiment to this purpose, that was made upon the eye of a dog on the anatomical theatre at Leyden. " upon a wound that had been given to his eye, the aqueous

Lect. VI. ous humor flowed so plentifully from it, that its membranes and coats appeared quite lank, flaccid and dry; and yet in six hours space the eye was again filled with the same aqueous humor; and that without the application of any medicines." with respect to that hollow of the eye, through which the rays pass to the retina, where the objects we see are painted, one might imagine it to be a matter of comparatively small importance, whether it were a little wider or a little narrower. yet it appears in fact and from observations made, that upon the slightest alteration in this respect, either by the contraction or dilatation of it, the greatest inconvenience would ensue. " how most exact then in the words of the poet is nature's frame! how wise the eternal mind!" how kind and friendly the formation of the eye in this respect, that the most useful dimension of this part should be so exactly and accurately preserved throughout the whole species! it is likewise highly worthy of remark, that in the eyes of

Brutes. brute animals there is a peculiar provision made for the usefulness, ease, safety and defence of this organ, according to the

par-

particular manner in which they are destined to live, and their being to be supported. thus we are told that in a frog, whose habitation is chiefly in watry places abounding with sedges and other plants, that have sharp points or edges, among which this animal is to be continually hopping about, there is a particular cartilage or membrane, with which it can at pleasure cover over the eye, without obstructing the sight of it; and thus defend itself from injury, this membrane being at once strong and transparent; and at pleasure too withdrawn, when there is no particular use or occasion for it. the same thing is observable in several sort of birds, who are destined to fly among plants and bushes, lest the prickles, twigs, leaves, or other parts, should wound or any way offend the eye. it is likewise very remarkable in horses and other animals, that are to feed for the most part on herbs and the grass of the field, and that they may the better choose their food, obliged to be long looking downward, that they are provided with what anatomists call the seventh muscle; a muscle not belonging to the eye of man, because there was no occasion for it; but with
great

LECT. VI. great wisdom and goodness made to be a part in the formation of the eye of these animals, that by means of it that wearisomeness and fatigue of the eye, which must otherways have necessarily ensued from this downward posture, might be prevented. " you will not, I hope, my little children, " think that these things are to be over- " looked or disregarded, because they are " illustrations drawn from the inferior part " of the creation, the mere animal tribe ; " since God is the former of these animals " as well as of man. and many excellent " uses are to be drawn from that goodness " and wisdom of the divine being, which " are so apparent in the production, struc- " ture and preservation of these inferior " creatures. thus for instance, if God " *takes care of oxen*, of sheep, nay, of frogs, " as is so apparent in the continued agencie " of his providence, from thence, my dear " child, you may infer, that you ought " not to use these brute creatures with " crueltie. for if God be continually pro- " viding for their ease and safety, in so " doing you must needs act in contrarietie " to him, which cannot surely be pleasing " in his sight, nor at all honorable to your- " self.

"self. and from hence you may infer, that if you cannot without displeasing him and acting in contradiction to the views of his providence, be barbarous and cruel in your treatment of this brutal tribe, you must to be sure offend him still more highly by using ill and cruelly any of your brethren of mankind. and then farther in the third place, if the kind providence of God is continually exercised in the preservation of these animals, you may certainly depend upon it that he will take care of you, and provide in the best manner for all your interests and concerns. I hope you remember that this is an argument made use of by your beloved saviour and redeemer himself. *if God take care of oxen, yea, and of the grass of the field, which to day is, and tomorrow is cast into the oven, how much more will he clothe you, o ye of little faith?*" but to return to the argument we were upon, and to use the words of an excellent writer in relation to it; " it must needs be incredible to any one that such a number of particular circumstances as are requisite in so great a matter as that of fight, fhould have concured and met in fo fmall a compafs as the fpace that contains the eye, by chance or by neceffarie caufes, without the leaft view or intention of a creating mind." but we have feen that there are not only the certain marks of defign and intention in it, but equally ftrong and certain marks likewife of a kind and benevolent intention. in this fingle inftance then, if we confider the conftant prefervation of the fame form and conftruction throughout the whole human fpecies and all the animal tribes, and that for a whole life; and that thus it has been for thoufands of years paft, if we reflect upon the innumerable benefits and advantages, pleafures and delights which we enjoy in confequence of this organ of vifion or fenfe of feeing, what a prodigioufly clear and fatisfying proof have we of the divine benignitie and goodnefs! but how much higher muft this proof arife, if we confider that the fame exquifite and friendly contrivance would appear upon an examination of all the other fenfes and organs; in thofe of hearing, tafte, fpeaking and the like, and in every part of nature whatfoever! upon fuch a furvey it muft

EXERCISES.

must appear altogether as absurd to deny the goodness of God as to deny his being. but as this is an attribute so essential to our happiness, as it is the foundation of all religion, and the only genuine ground of devotion, without the conviction of which possessing our minds, we could only dread omnipotence and be astonished at infinite wisdom, I propose to pursue my reflexions upon it, and to lay before you some different views of the argument upon which we found our belief of it as belonging to the sovereign mind.

Devotion.

LECTURE VII.

WE are now treating upon the goodness of God. and it is observed in the scriptures that *the earth is full of it.* "you remember I hope, my good children, "the passage I refer to. yes, sir, it is in "the thirty-third Psalm: *the Lord loveth* "*righteousness and judgement; the earth is* "*full of the goodness of the Lord.* and do "you not think that by that expression "the

"the pfalmift might mean, that in the
"conftant, regular and plentiful produc-
"tions of the *earth* God hath given to
"mankind a moft vifible difplay and clear
"demonftration of his goodnefs? or do
"you imagine his meaning in this expref-
"fion to have been, that every thing which
"comes within the notice of the inhabi-
"tants of the earth, the whole ftructure
"and formation of the world, and all the
"ftated and orderly appearances of it, are
"fo many difplays of that goodnefs? this
"latter is the more extenfive idea, and
"will naturally include the other. I fup-
"pofe then it is that which you would pre-
"fer. this however, I may venture to
"affure you of, that in that one particu-
"lar comprehended under this general
"expreffion of the pfalmift, which I have
"already hinted at, according to this more
"extenfive interpretation of it, the pro-
"duction I mean of the fruits of the earth,
"and the provifion that is made for the
"continual fupplie and regular fucceffion
"of them, is contained a very ftrong deci-
"five illuftration of the argument which
"we are now upon; the proof I mean of
"the divine goodnefs. you have been
"already

"already told how curioufly and wonder- Lect. VII.
"fully the body of man, as well as that of
"all the animals belonging to this earthly
"or terraqueous globe has been formed.
"a terraqueous globe this earth is fome-
"times called; becaufe it confifts of fea
"and waters as well as land. and this fo
"admirable ftructure of our bodies we
"have infifted upon as a moft demonftra-
"tive argument not only of defign, but
"of kind and gracious defign, that is
"to a creating and fovereign deitie to be
"afcribed. but pray, my good children,
"what would you have thought, fuppofing
"man to have been made juft in the fame
"manner he now is, endued with all the
"fame organs, limbs, fenfes, and animal
"appetites, which he now poffeffes; and
"that the ftructure of the mere animals,
"the birds, the beafts and infects, had
"been juft what it is at prefent; but yet
"that no provifion had been made in the
"fyftem of nature for the fupport and Friendly
"fuftenance in thefe feveral claffes of this adaptations in nature,
"animal frame? indeed, upon that fuppo-
"fition, my idea of the divine goodnefs
"would be very much obfcured. becaufe
"I find upon my own perpetual experi-
"ence,

Lect. VII.
illustration of.

"ence, that notwithstanding all the won-
"derful formation of my body, it stands
"in need of daily support and refreshment,
"and that the want of these would soon
"have subjected me to a great deal of
"pain and miserie, and at length have
"terminated in the destruction and disso-
"lution of that animal constitution that is
"belonging to me. you seem then, my
"dear child, to apprehend, unless I mis-
"take your meaning, that man might
"have been formed just as he is, with all
"these wonderful contrivances and marks
"of skill in his bodily frame and contex-
"ture, and yet that in this very frame and
"structure of him there might have been
"no proof at all of the goodness of his
"creator, but rather of some contrarie
"disposition in that being. is it possible
"that the case could have been so? if you
"please, sir, I will venture to express my
"thoughts more fully upon that head; and
"then refer them wholly to your judge-
"ment, hoping, or rather indeed not
"doubting, but that you will be so kind as
"to correct my error, if you find me to
"have fallen into any. well, you will
"procede then upon that condition. I
                                    "will.

EXERCISES.

LECT. VII.

" will. I was much delighted with the
" account you gave me, upon the laſt op-
" portunitie I had of converſing with you
" upon this head, of the curious ſtructure
" and fabric of the eye. but might not
" mine eye have been made juſt as it is, and
" yet the quantitie of light have been far
" too great to have anſwered the ends of
" ſight? nay, might it not have been ſo
" exceſſive as to have put me to the ſe-
" vereſt torture in conſequence of that
" very conſtruction of mine eye, which
" you were then inſiſting upon; and by
" this means I ſhould not only have been
" deſtitute of all the pleaſures of ſeeing,
" but likewiſe have lived in exceſſive tor-
" ment and miſerie. or might not the
" objects with which I had been ſurround-
" ed, and which by the light I had diſ-
" covered, have been odious and hateful to
" my ſight, troubleſome and afflictive to
" the eye, and a continued ſource of terri-
" fying and frightful ideas, and of uneaſie
" and painful ſenſations? indeed, my
" child, I muſt own that there ſeems to be
" no direct and abſolute impoſſibilitie in
" theſe ſuppoſitions. and you think that,
" had this been really the caſe, it would
" have

"have appeared that your eye, instead of being formed with any kind or benevolent design, had been rather made and contrived purely for the sake of rendering you liable to all this torture. indeed, sir, I see not how I could have made any other conclusion. you told me likewise that my ear was very admirably formed for hearing. but what, if all the sounds that were presented to it, instead of being what they now are, had been continually terrifying and alarming, like so many bursting claps of thunder, and that by this means I had been almost distracted and rendered incapable either of attending to any of the concerns, or enjoying any of the blessings of life? indeed, child, I am ready to own with you, that had this been the case, you had better have been without this curious organ of hearing. and that it is not, is only to be ascribed to the pure and absolute benevolence of that sovereign mind which created all things. in like manner, dear sir, as things are at present, I am so far from being sorry that my animal frame stands in need of continual sustenance and refreshment, "that

" that I find a great deal of present, and
" I hope innocent, satisfaction, in par-
" taking of the *food* that is *convenient for*
" *me*, besides the many lasting blessings
" that accrue from it. and I am often
" very thankful to God, that there is such
" provision made in the structure of my
" body for the taking in and digestion of
" my food, and for promoting the nou-
" rishment of my body by it, that the
" necessary support of my nature, instead
" of being any burden, is on the contrary
" itself one of the gratifications belonging
" to my animal frame. I often think too
" that there is something very entertaining
" in that vast varietie of methods by which
" my fellow-creatures all around me are
" continually employed in providing for
" themselves and their families these necef-
" farie refreshments of their being, and in
" the success, with which for the most part
" these labors are attended. but alas, how
" miserable would have been the case, if
" notwithstanding the wise formation of
" those particular parts and organs that
" minister to the uses and ends of nourish-
" ment, there had been no provision made
" in the scene of nature for a continual
                                              " and

Lect. VII. "and plentiful supply of that nourish-
"ment! what a dreadful thing must it
"have been to be able to eat, to be want-
"ing to eat, and yet to have no food pro-
"vided for us; to have had it wholly and
"absolutely out of our power to procure
"any; that all mankind should have been
"in this perishing condition, by some
"means or another continually starting up
"into the world with all these appetites
"about them, only to pine for a while in
"extremest miserie, and then to expire.
"this surely would have shewn crueltie
"and not goodness in the being that made
"them, if any such there were. that in-
"deed must be allowed. but then if the
"direct contrarie to all this appears to be
"the real state of things; if the construc-
"tion and order of the world around us is
"so admirably adapted to the formation of
"our own bodies, as to be a continual sup-
"plie to them of nourishment, refresh-
"ment, gratification and pleasure, then I
"suppose you will readily allow, my child,
"that the proof of goodness in deitie is
"so far complete, and the argument in
"support of it prodigiously heightened and
"made to appear in a vastly stronger point
"of

"of view." now this is indeed exactly the case. as the eye is so admirably formed for seeing, so the light, with which we are continually surrounded, and which is perpetually presented to it, is exactly such for degree and quantity and continuance, as to be prodigiously refreshing and comfortable to the sight, instead of being in the least degree painful or disagreeable. and yet how easily might it have happened otherwise, had there not been some highly intelligent and kindly designing mind, who first placed the earth and the heavenly bodies in such an exact situation one towards another, and continually preserves that position that is best adapted for our comfort, ease and pleasure in this particular? how small a deviation from this order of nature would involve us in the most confounding perplexitie and horror? and whence is it, think you, that such a deviation should never happen? how can we account for it but by a divine and continually presiding providence? perpetual light, even tho' it were in no greater a degree than that which we have at midday, would perhaps be as great an inconvenience as even total darkness itself, to which after a while it would probably reduce us

by

Lect. VII. by its too powerful and inceffant operation upon the vifual organ. darknefs therefore is a relief to the eye, as light is the comfort and joy of it. it would likewife have been an extreme detriment and prejudice to vifion, and muft in a great meafure have defeated the defign of it, if not wholly deftroyed it, had night been fucceded in an inftant by the fulleft blaze of day. and it is a moft admirably kind contrivance in the fyftem of the world, that light both comes and goes gradually, and not inftantaneoufly. and the fame exactnefs of kind and benevolent intention is equally obfervable in that degree of heat which we receive from the fun, and which invigorates the whole animal and vegetable fyftem. Mr. Keil tells us that the great comet which appeared in the year 1680, had approched fo near to the fun, as to be made by the heat of it three thoufand times hotter than red-hot iron. how fmall a degree of fuch an acquired heat, additional to what the earth ftatedly partakes of in confequence of its exact pofition in the planetary fyftem, would be enough to throw the whole of our orb into the moft dreadful diforder and confufion! what a benignitie and goodnefs

muft

EXERCISES.

must then be apparent in that original contrivance and perpetual order, by virtue of which we are so far from being subject to any inconvenience of this kind, that we constantly enjoy such a degree of heat from the sun, as invigorates every part of nature, and brings its various productions year after year to their exactly wished-for maturitie and perfection! but still notwithstanding this exact position of the earth, how dreadful would be our condition, were it not for the air or atmosphere, thro' the medium of which the rays of light are transmited, and which is formed of the exactest consistencie for that purpose? but the air likewise, as it is of absolute necessitie for the transition of light, and answers the most kind and friendly intention of nature, or rather I should say, and would be understood to mean, of the great author of nature in this respect, being in itself absolutely necessary for the support of animal life, what a perpetual goodness is apparent in it's being so exactly adapted to the purposes of respiration? for by experiments made in the air-pump it has appeared, that were the air we breathe, only in a small degree more compressed or thicker than it is, is, or on the other hand, in a small degree only more rarified or thinner in it's consistencie, it would be so far from contributing to the support of animal life, that it would indeed destroy it. but yet, notwithstanding this admirable position of the earth with respect to the sun, and this exact aptitude in the densitie of the air for the transmission of it's light and the purposes of respiration, all would be in vain, and man in this respect a miserable creature, or else very soon cease to be an inhabitant of this earthly globe, were there not some constant provision made in nature for keeping this latter in motion, in order to prevent it's putrefaction. if this were not done, as an ingenious writer expresses it, " instead of refreshing and animating, it " would suffocate and poison all the world." to this admirably serve the perpetual gales and frequent storms of wind. we value much and justly, the late invention of ventilators, and are very thankful to those who have favored the world with this ingenious and most useful invention for clearing ships and other crouded structures of the foul and noxious air that has been contracted, and introducing that which is fresh

and

and wholesome. this however is only a very faint and shadowy imitation of nature. a mere trifling and despicable benefit, great as it is in itself, when compared with the grand provision in this respect made by the sovereign intelligence; by means of which the whole system of air is at once with the greatest facilitie, and without the least trouble to the inhabitants of the world continually cleansed and purified. and yet how apt are we to employ our thoughts and conversation in the admiration of these human inventions, the imperfect copies only of nature, while we overlook the benevolent and wise intention of the supreme opificer, who with such exuberant goodness has formed, contrived and adjusted every thing for the benefit and good of man? " and
" does it not, my children, give you a
" very high and exalted idea of the divine
" goodness, to think of the amazing, in-
" expressible number of mankind, and of
" the inferior creatures, that have ever
" since the creation been subsisting in con-
" sequence of these happily established
" laws of nature continually upheld by the
" never-ceasing exertion of the great cre-
" ator?" " the earth, as we have seen," says
the

LECT. VII. the Pfalmift, "is full of the goodnefs of "the Lord." and if we do but confider the magnitude of this earth thus replete with goodnefs, what a' large, extenfive idea muft we needs form of that goodnefs itfelf? the bulk or folid contents of our globe is no lefs than two hundred and fixty thoufand millions of miles; and all this prodigioufly wide extenfive fcene quite *filled* with " goodnefs;" an innumerable varietie of birds, beafts, infects, reptiles, fifhes, in every clafs of which, and in every individual of thefe claffes the moft exquifite workmanfhip and contrivance apparent for the accommodation of the animal according to his particular habitation and mode of living. add to all this the rich and plentiful productions of the earth in its minerals, vegetables and fruits, in the formation and growth of all which there are the moft evident marks of a kind and benevolent intention. every thing is fitted for bringing them to their proper degree of perfection, and in all thefe productions there is nothing but what has it's admirable ufes. this or that upon an hafty view may feem trifling or it may be noxious to us; but yet upon a nearer examination is
found

Globe.

found to be useful. thus we are told that the common thistle, which grows by the highway, is even more useful when reduced to ashes, than any other thistle whatsoever in the making of glass, from whence we derive such a number of conveniencies. ": does a nettle sting," says one, " it is to " secure so good a medicine from the rapes " of children and cattle. does the bramble " cumber a garden, it makes the better " hedge, or if it chance to prick the owner, " it will tear the thief. if hemlock be poison " to man, it is physic to some animals, " and food to another." nay, even to man himself it sometimes proves extremely beneficial by a proper mode of preparation, and being taken in a certain quantitie only. even in the very color of the grass of the earth, of the leaves of the trees, and the vegetables of the ground, we have an admirable and very convincing proof of the goodness of the creator ; it being that very one which is most of all agreeable and pleasant to the eye, and which it longest endures ; and, if any other than that of green had been the color of nature, we should soon have found the highest inconveniencies arising from it.

But

Lect. VII.

Other worlds.

But then this earth is far from being the only scene of nature, in which the divine goodness exerts and displays itself. from the discoveries that have been made by astronomical observations, it seems very evident that the other planets belonging to the same solar system with our earth, are like it inhabited. provision seems to have been made for that purpose according to their respective distances from the sun. and from a provision of this kind actually discovered to us, compared with what we see throughout the whole globe which we ourselves inhabit, we may justly upon the principles of analogie, and with the fairest probabilitie, conclude that the same kind, gracious and benevolent order prevails throughout each of these distinct and separate worlds. and as according to the like observations the fixed stars are probably supposed to be so many suns having a planetarie system belonging to each, how prodigiously, according to this just and natural reasoning or ground of analogie, is our idea of the divine goodness extended! however, by considering this earth of ours alone, and attending to that prodigious bulk of it, which has been already spoken of, and

the

EXERCISES.

LECT. VII.

the inceſſant proofs of goodneſs that have been apparent in it ever ſince the creation, and in every part of it, how can we properly expreſs our idea of ſo much goodneſs actually proved and appearing throughout ſo vaſt an extent of ſpace and duration, but by calling it infinite? thus from the *actual* effects of it are we taught to conceive of this goodneſs as being ſo great, ſo free, ſo permanent, ſo exuberant and overflowing, that it is impoſſible we ſhould have too high a dependance upon it, or raiſe our notions and apprehenſions too far concerning it. it muſt needs appear from theſe conſiderations, only to be a goodneſs calling for our moſt elevated and fervent praiſes, and laying a foundation for our everlaſting triumphs. ſurrounded as we are with *demonſtrations* of a goodneſs like this, it is not enough to ſay that downright atheiſm muſt needs be the groſſeſt ſtupiditie. but a very lamentable degree of indolence and lethargie muſt it implie in our intellectual and moral powers, not to have our ſouls moſt deeply impreſſed with an affecting, lively ſenſe of this divine and all-ſuſtaining love. we are to judge, we ſay, of the goodneſs of a man by his actions

G

LECT. VII. and conduct. in the divine actions and conduct then, what full and satisfying proof have we of that goodness, which is divine? of the degree of a fellow-creature's goodness we judge by the number and importance of his beneficent actions. according to this manner of determining, what language can be too strong, or rather what words suffice, to express the true idea of the benignitie and beneficence of that God, who is *good to all, and whose tender mercies are over all his works?* o then *praise the Lord with me, and let us exalt his name together.* let us not look upon our acknowlegements of the divine goodness only as a decent compliment paid to the author of our natures; but let us offer them cordially and affectionately, and with a devotion corresponding as nearly as possible to the incontestable evidence we have of it.

A SERMON.

A SERMON.

Monday, Dec. 25.

1 Tim. iii. 16.

And without controversie great is the mysterie of godliness: God was manifest in the flesh, justified in the spirit, seen of angels, preached unto the Gentiles, believed on in the world, received up into glorie.

"LET no man, says bishop Hall, go about to entertain the thought of the great mysterie of godliness, but with a ravished heart, an heart filled with a gracious composition of love and joy and wonder." tho' therefore much has been said in the world, and this too with great heat and eagerness, concerning the meaning of the word mysterie, yet it is far from

being

Sermon. being my defign to enter upon any examination of that debate, or any confiderations of that kind at prefent. in reference to our text, in which you perceive the word to occur, I fhall leave every one to underftand by it almoft what he pleafes. nor do I apprehend the critical meaning of the word to be a matter of any great importance here, fo long as we rightly underftand the thing that is denominated by it; namely, the fyftem of chriftianitie. here is fomething called a myfterie. now whatever be the meaning of this word, yet the apoftle immediately procedes to give you a very particular defcription of that which he calls fo. and this defcription we may be very well able to underftand, without determining why he calls it fo, or being able precifely to adjuft the fignification of fuch a word. fome by the word myfterie feem to intend that which is totally incomprehenfible, or a mere collection of words, which have no meaning at all in them. but it is plain this cannot be the interpretation of it here; on account of that clear, explicit and very intelligible defcription, given of what is called a myfterie. by this term, however, may well enough be denoted

fome-

something of which we know a great deal, but concerning which there is a great deal more that still remains to be known. and in this sense christianitie may very justly be called a mysterie, without at all derogating from the excellencie of it. nay, the expression does indeed imply such a superior and consummate excellencie in it, as is not to be at once, but only in the gradual advance and progress of the understanding fully comprehended by the mind of man. under this notion of christianitie the apostle himself has given us a very exact and lively representation of it in another of his epistles; that I mean to the Ephesians. he there informs them of its being his tender affectionate prayer to God in their behalf, that " he would grant unto them
" according to the riches of his glorie, to
" be strengthened with might by his spirit
" in the inner man, that Christ might
" dwell in their hearts by faith, that they
" being rooted and grounded in love, may
" be able to comprehend with all saints
" what is the breadth and length and depth
" and height, and to know the love of
" Christ, which passeth knowlege." here you see the apostle supposes that there is a

great

great deal to be known concerning chriftianitie, even " the breadth and length and " depth and height" of it, and yet that on another account it " paffeth know-" lege." that is to fay, there is fo much to be known concerning it, that we cannot even by the moft diligent ftudie attain to the whole of that knowlege in the prefent life. it paffes the limits of our prefent powers. but this is very far from being a reafon againft the ftudie of the gofpel. on the contrarie, it gives us a very pleafing view of this employment. it points out chriftianitie to us as a copious, inexhauftible fubject, in our contemplation of which we fhall always be fure to meet with fomething, that will be ftill farther entertaining and fatisfactorie to the mind, beyond the amount of that we have already difcovered in relation to it. we can never grow wearie of contemplating a fubject, which is fo great and noble as to excede the full comprehenfion even of the moft improved and cultivated underftanding during this ftate of mortalitie. on this account then chriftianitie may juftly by St. Paul in our text be called a myfterie. that likewife is very naturally ftyled a myfterie, which appears

pears even by what we do know and moſt clearly perceive concerning it, to carry in it ſuch an eminent degree of dignitie, excellencie, uſefulneſs, worth and importance, as cannot but excite our higheſt admiration, ſurpaſſing, as it may ſeem to do, all that has ever yet been diſcovered in the kind, or that imagination itſelf could have ſuggeſted. and on this farther account how juſtly may Chriſtianitie be ſaid to be myſterious? what an aſtoniſhing ſcene of love does it exhibit? how does it ſurpriſe and amaze our faculties by that exuberance of goodneſs to which we owe it! and with what conſummate and admirable wiſdom is it as a religious inſtitution or moral ſtructure contrived and modeled for promoting the everlaſting intereſts of mankind! " o the depths both of the wiſ-
" dom and of the knowlege of God! how
" unſearchable are his judgments, and his
" ways paſt finding out!" the grandeur and excellencie of this religious ſyſtem are never enough to be admired; never can they be ſufficiently extolled in our praiſes, thankſgivings and adorations on account of them. well then, for theſe two reaſons in conjunction, may chriſtianitie not only be ſtyled a myſterie, but a *great* one too. it

is a system that furnishes us with a copious and inexhaustible fund of contemplation, and at the same time presents to our view in the several particulars of it, objects the most surprizing, full of dignitie, excellencie and beautie, and beyond all comparison or adequate conception, interesting, great and illustrious. but what does the apostle mean by saying, "*without con-troverfie* great is the mysterie of godliness?" by the connexion to which I refer you, as well as by the import of the original word here made use of, it should seem to have been his intention in this expression to remind both Timothy and us of that high degree of clear and unexceptionable evidence, with which the publication of the gospel as a divinely authorised system of religion was accompanied; that "demonstration of the spirit" which attended it, and in consequence of which it came after a while to be established over all the world as a doctrine, not only apparently interesting and important, but confessedly true and well-attested. but by no means are we to pass over that other character, which the apostle gives us of "this great mysterie." it is a "mysterie of *godliness.*"

far

far is he from speaking of it in this lan- {Sermon.}
guage as if it were a thing at all surprising
that godliness should be the design of christianitie, or the great end that was aimed at
by the publication and establishment of it
in the world. from the essential perfections
indeed of the divine being, we may most
safely conclude on the other hand, that this
only could be the ultimate view of it. but
the apostle's intention here is to impress
our minds with the sentiment, that as godliness is, and necessarily must be the great
end and ultimate design of the gospel, so it
is in the whole fabric and construction of
it most *admirably* fited to answer this end;
that it is a dispensation in the nature and
tendencie of it most highly efficacious for this
purpose; a scheme in the best manner possible, and with the most exquisite skill contrived for promoting the interest of pietie
in the heart and in the world.

But let us now procede to the particulars
of it as here specified by the apostle. " great
" then," he says, " is the mysterie of god-
" liness: God was manifest in the flesh ;"
or, as we might with greater emphasis and
a more exact conformitie to the original
read, *a* " God was manifest in the flesh,
" justified

"justified in the spirit, seen of angels, preached unto the Gentiles, believed on in the world, received up into glorie." "a God," says the apostle, in the first place, "was manifest in the flesh." it was not God the sovereign father. "him no man hath seen or can see." it is one of the peculiar attributes of his nature to be invisible to mortal eye. but the God here spoken of was " manifest in the flesh." he was "seen" of men as well as by angels. it was not then the God and father of our Lord Jesus Christ that is here said to have been " manifested in the flesh." nor yet was it on the other hand any of those inferior beings the angels, any one of which might nevertheless upon becoming incarnate, in order to deliver some special message of grace and mercie to mankind, and giving authentic attestations of his heavenly mission, have been naturally enough styled "a God," since beings much below them, even magistrates and earthly princes, are in scripture so characterised and denominated. but it is not, I say, any one of this sublime, angelical order that is spoken of here in our text; but a being inconceivably exalted above them, even God the son, or the God

God Chrift. he it is, he that " in the be-
" gining was with God, and" from the
begining " was God." he it is that " was
" manifeft in the flefh, but juftified" the
apoftle adds " in the fpirit," by way of
contraft to the former expreffion, and fo
both claufes are to be taken in conjunction,
in order to our entering fully into the fenfe
and meaning of them. " a God manifeft
" in the flefh," might fome be ready to
afk; how can that be! how could divinitie
and humanitie thus coincide and meet together! why truly, fays the apoftle, " in
" the flefh," in the external circumftances
and mere worldly condition of the perfon I
am here fpeaking of, fo little was there of
this divinitie apparent, that he was on the
contrarie numbered amongft the meaneft of
the people. he was not only " in the
" flefh," but manifefted alfo in the loweft
circumftances of humanitie. he was not
only a man, " but a man of forrows, and
" acquainted with grief." others of mankind, as it was declared concerning him in
prophecy, " hid their faces from him" in
contempt, far from " feeing any form or
" comelinefs in him, " or any beautie,"
that they " fhould defire him;" they
" defpifed

"despised and rejected him." so little appearance or manifestation was there of any inhabiting divinitie in the external circumstances of him, who was thus "manifest in the flesh." nevertheless, "by the spirit," by that spirit of infallible truth with which he spoke, and that spirit of power by which this truth was attested, was his claim to divinitie, and our ascriptions of it to him fully justified." by "this spirit" likewise was he "justified," or his character asserted, not only as being in the original honors of his nature exalted above angels and arch-angels, and the most glorious, elevated beings of all the heavenly hierarchie, but also as the prophet of God, and as the appointed teacher, instructor and savior of mankind. these are so many characters, which he himself assumed, whilst here upon earth, and which his apostles afterwards did in the most solemn and public manner insist upon as belonging to him. for this reason it was that "his name was "called Jesus, because he should save his people," the people among whom he was born, as likewise all who should profess themselves his disciples, and make the proper improvement of his religion, of whatever

ever age or country, " from their sins." Sermon.
and in conformitie to a name at once so
interesting, so honorable and so endearing,
he declared himself to be come into the
world that he might be " the light of it,"
and that God had " anointed him to preach
" the gospel to the poor, to heal the
broken hearted, to preach deliverance to
the captives," the captives of sin and the
slaves of vice, and recovering of sight " to
" the blind," the ignorant and deluded in
matters of religion, and in relation to the
true happiness of man. to " set at libertie
" them that are bruised, to preach the ac-
" ceptable year of the Lord." and in pro-
phecie it had been said of him most suitably
to such a name, that in consequence of his
appearance, " the people, who sat in dark-
" ness should see great light, and that to
" them who sat in the region and shadow
" of death, light should spring up ;" of so
much estimation is light in the account
which the scriptures give us of the gospel-
salvation. a plain sign, that we ourselves
have not a right apprehension of it, when we
can allow ourselves in despising the *light* of
divine truth, and can be content to live in
almost the grossest ignorance of it, rather
than

than be at the pains required in order to our being acquainted with it. in correspondence likewise to this name or character, with which even at his birth he had been invested, he declares that when he should "be lifted up on the cross," this should be in order to "draw all men unto "him," and that he might by expiring upon it "give his life a ransom for many;" and that the blood, which there flowed from his pierced hands and feet and side, was "shed for many for the remission of "sins." accordingly he elsewhere assumes to himself the power or authoritie of giving eternal life. "I give," he says, "unto my "sheep eternal life, and they shall never "perish, neither shall any pluck them out "of mine hand. my father, who gave "them me, is greater than all; and none "is able to pluck them out of my father's "hand. I and my father are one." as it is he that gave them to me, we are in this respect one. and the promised salvation of my sheep is secure in mine hands, because it is so in the hands of that sovereign deitie, who has commited them to my care; and who is too good, too wise, too mightie, ever to permit that trust to be defeated.

defeated. such are the powers laid claim to even by him, who, when he took upon him our nature, appeared in " the form of " a servant:" but yet in all these claims has he been " justified by the spirit;" that is, by those " signs and wonders and divers " gifts of the holy ghost," from which is arising so ample a testimony to the truth of his mission, and consequently of these claims. our savior likewise, tho' according to his appearance or manifestation " in the " flesh," he " made himself of no reputa- " tion," yet how fully was he "*justified*" to the impartial and discerning eye by that spirit of pietie and love, which animated all his conduct, in which we have exhibited to our view a character not only *justified* from reproche, not only raised above contempt, but appearing in the highest degree venerable, fair and lovely. well may he be said to have been justified in the spirit, in whose *spirit* there was absolutely " no guile." not the least defect in point of moral temper, but every thing that was perfective of it. in the character likewise, which he assumed as the prophet of the most high God, how amply did he *justifie* his claim, not only by the miraculous
powers

powers which he exerted, but likewife by the very *spirit* itfelf and genius of that religion, which they were intended to confirm. a religion fo worthy of God, in the higheft degree honorable to all his perfections, and in the moft direct, immediate and efficacious manner conducing to the welfare and fupreme felicitie of man, and thus by its native *spirit* and intrinfic excellence recommending itfelf and its divine author to our warmeft approbation and moft cordial acceptance. it is added, " feen of angels." but where, it may be afked, lies the wonder of that? had he not been *seen* of them before? yes; but never " in flefh." it was a new and aftonifhing fight to thefe angelic beings to *see* this God " manifefted in " the flefh;" him, whofe heavenly dignitie fo far fuperior to their own, they had been wont to gaze at with fo much wonder and holy admiration; this very being they now with equal aftonifhment *see* taking up his abode amongft mortal men, defpifed, reviled, perfecuted, afflicted, expofed to all manner of labors, fatigues, pains and tortures. and here, as it fhould feem, lies the force and emphafis of this claufe in our text, it is faid indeed, only " feen of angels."

but

but the apostle knew that every reader must immediately add in his own reflexions; seen with wonder, seen with admiration and surprize. and the sentiment was probably introduced in order to heighten and aggrandize our ideas of the condescension of the son of God in becoming incarnate. nor could any thing have been more naturally adapted to this purpose than the pointing it out as being the object of wondering contemplation to these high angelic orders. but he was also in the fourth place, " preached " unto the Gentiles." his manifestation " in the flesh" was intended to be a general diffusive good; and to carry in it a most lively display, specimen, emblem and proof of that sovereign, divine and universal goodness to which we are indebted for it. and this, tho' it cannot but appear to us as being in the highest degree agreeable to all our natural notions and most obvious reasonings concerning the divine perfections, was matter of no little astonishment to the Jews. they were strangely limited and confined in their affections towards mankind, and were therefore disposed to ascribe the like limitations even to the divine benevolence itself; to look upon the Gentiles, all men

but

but themselves, as being in a manner abandoned and forsaken of God, and their own nation only, as being his favorites and the objects of his delight; insomuch that they never once thought that the Messiah was to be the savior of any besides the Jews. and it was one of their greatest objections to his gospel, that he professed to come into the world that he might be the redeemer of all. and for this reason it is expresly spoken of in another part of this apostle's writings as a mysterie; that "the Gentiles should "be fellow heirs and of the same bodie" with the Jews, "and partakers" as well as they "of his promise in Christ by the gos- "pel." a mysterie, which, how unwelcome soever it might be to Jewish prejudices, partialitie, selfishness and bigotrie, we ourselves have the highest reason to rejoice in, and with the devoutest affection to be thankful for. since it is in consequence of this very dispensation that we now enjoy such inestimable and glorious privileges; and have Christ amongst us in order to the having "Christ within us as the hope of "glorie." but farther fifthly, he was not only "preached unto the Gentiles," but in consequence of this actually "believed on
"in

"in the world." we call that amidst the events and occurrences in life "a myste-"rie," which, according to all human appearance and probabilities, was very unlikely to have happened. this particular clause of our text therefore is most naturally introduced by the apostle when speaking of christianitie under the notion in general or idea of a mysterie. it was a scheme or dispensation that carried in it one entire contradiction to all the prevaling customs and established modes of the world. "to "the Jews it was a stumbling-block, and "to the Greeks foolishness." all the wisdom and power, all the passions and prejudices of mankind were armed against it. so that according to all human appearances, "God manifest in the flesh" might have been "preached to the Gentiles," but could scarce have been "believed on in the "world." yet mightie was the power of God to the "pulling down of these strong "holds." and therefore was he not only "preached unto the Gentiles," but likewise "believed on in the world." he that during his abode upon earth was called in contempt "the son of a carpenter," reviled as a "glutton and a wine-biber, accused

"as

SERMON. " as a blafphemer, treated as a madman," and charged with " having a devil," and at length put to death thro' the prevalence of enraged and virulent malice as a malefactor, was afterwards " believed on in the " world," and that not in fome fmall part of it only, but throughout every region, territorie and quarter of the earth, as " a " God manifeft in the flefh;" had every-where churches founded in his name, folemnities appointed to his honor, and hearts devoted to his fervice. " fo mightily did " the word of God prevail." with fo much reafon may we fay, " this is the lord's " doing, and it is *marvelous* in our eyes." but to heighten and complete the grand idea, which it was the apoftle's defign in this paffage to give us of the fplendor and dignitie of the gofpel-fcheme, and of the amazing glories that centered in the perfon of its adorable author; he adds in the fixth and laft place, " received up into glorie." once he was manifefted " in the flefh," appeared in the loweft form of humanitie, and " being found in fafhion as a man, he " humbled himfelf." humiliation indeed! for he " became obedient unto death, even " the death of the crofs." but behold how

foon

soon the scene is changed. direct your *Sermon.* wondering eyes and astonished hearts to the honors with which he is now invested. he has been long since "received into glorie. "God has highly exalted him, and given "him a name above every name, that at "the name of Jesus every knee should "bow." he that was "despised and re- "jected of men," is now adored by angels, and seated at the "right hand" of the sovereign father's throne." that, said our savior once, while here on earth, which is highly esteemed "amongst men, is abomination in "the sight of God." here we see with what abundant reason we may reverse the maxim, and say, that which is despised and of no reputation in the sight of men, carries in it the highest value, merit and acceptableness in the sight of God. reflecting methinks upon those heavenly glories, with which the savior of the world is now invested, our gratitude for all the condescensions of his wonderful incarnation and dying love should instantly break forth into songs of congratulation. BLESSED JESUS, we rejoice in these thy triumphs, in these thy splendid honors, in that illustrious crown thou wearest, and which commands the
                              reverence

reverence and subjection of all the angelic hosts. we join their songs. we gladly take our part in their hosanna's, and say with them: " worthy art thou, the lamb that " was slain, to receive riches and blessing " and honor and glorie and power." we adore the divine munificence and love, which has thus gloriously rewarded that unwearied compassion of thine, which was exerted for our sakes. and by these rejoicing, grateful sentiments we feel ourselves, indulge thou condescending savior, indulge us in the thought, we feel ourselves to become partakers in thy renown. but yet after another sort, not exclusive of this our present kind of joy, but additional to it, and perfective of it, we hope ere long to be sharing in thy bliss and honors. for by the gracious promises of thy word we are taught to believe that thou art " en-
" tered within the veil as our forerunner." this " hope thou hast set before us," that " it might be the anchor of our souls both " sure and stedfast." and in thy life-time here on earth thou wast pleased to pray for us in these encouraging, animating terms ; that we " might be with thee, where thou " art, to behold the glorie which thou
" hadst

" hadſt with the father before the world
" was." bleſſed Jeſus, our ſouls are aſpiring after and longing for it." · " come
" Lord Jeſus, come quickly." and as an
earneſt of this our promiſed inheritance,
o that thou mayeſt now be *manifeſted* to
each one of us by the efficacious influence
of thy goſpel upon our hearts. " take
" unto thyſelf thy great power" and reign
within us. let us not content ourſelves
with hearing this bleſſed goſpel " preached,"
as thro' the indulgent grace of heaven is
ſtill the privilege enjoyed among us of the
Gentile ſtock. but may its vital influences
be feeled by every power and affection of
our natures. and as we are now profeſſing
in the ſight of God and by the ſolemnities
of his worſhip, to rejoice that thy name is
" believed on. in the world," let us manifeſt the ſinceritie of theſe our ſolemn profeſſions, by ſuffering this faith to " work"
in our hearts " by love." never, never let
it be ſaid, to the aſtoniſhment of the whole
angelic world, that the only-begotten of
the moſt high did " manifeſt himſelf in
fleſh" purely and alone for our ſakes, and
that yet we have deſpiſed the offers even of
ſuch condeſcending love, and have choſen
rather

rather to renounce our savior than our lusts! and as we profess to emulate the angelic host in the celebration of thy praises, and to make it our ambition to be *hereafter* like them, may it be the matter of our most diligent and attentive studie to be like to them, and like to thee in puritie and innocence of soul even *now*; knowing as we do, that for this end thou " gavest thyself for " us, to redeem us from all iniquitie, and " to purifie unto thyself a peculiar peo- " ple, zealous of good works," and that " without holiness no man shall see the " Lord."

LECTURE VIII.

WE have already endevored to give you fome account of thofe proofs, which we have of the divine goodnefs in the vifible works of the creation; their order and their general tendencie to utilitie and happinefs. and I think thefe proofs muft needs appear to thofe, who duly, diligently and impartially attend to them, to amount to a ftrict and proper demonftration of fuch a goodnefs in the deitie, as we and the reft of our fellow-creatures of mankind may fafely confide in with refpect to all our higheft interefts, and by the exertion of which we may firmly believe thefe will be in the moft effectual manner provided for. but there are ftill other arguments to be infifted upon, which afford a very high degree of additional evidence in the point before us. and furely we cannot have too much; or be content that any thing tending to heighten the proof fhould be omited. it is here, properly fpeaking, that our all is at ftake. if God be indeed infinitely and unchangeably good,

H

Lec. VIII. good, then may I address myself to you all; "and to you in particular, my good
"children; and assure you that *all things*
"*are yours. whether Paul or Apollos or Ce-*
"*phas,* any of your fellow-creatures, with
"whom you may have particular con-
"nexions; *or the world, or life or death,*
"*or things present, or things to come;* all
"*are yours.* that is, by this presiding and
"all-directing goodness of the deitie, they
"will be made to turn to your account.
"and you may be, as St. Paul declares he
"was, fully *perſuaded that neither death nor*
"*life, nor angels nor principalities nor pow-*
"*ers, nor things present nor things to come,*
"*nor heighth nor depth nor any other creature,*
"*shall be able to separate us from this love of*
"*God, which is in Chriſt Jeſus our Lord;*"
having by this great and most illustrious messenger of peace and mercie been so amply
displayed and so signally ratified and confirmed. I will therefore procede in my endevor to corroborate the belief of this
divine goodness by such other arguments as
I just now refered to, and which have not
as yet been insisted upon in this our stated
inquirie, relative to that and other subjects
naturally connected with it. now there is

something like what is called an argument *a priori* that may be produced to this purpose; that is, there is an argument to be drawn in proof of the divine goodness independent of any actual effects of it, as discerned by us, and which is wholly founded upon those other attributes, which we cannot but ascribe to the divine and sovereign nature. such for instance as the divine power and wisdom, and the independent happiness of the divine being. the latter of these we shall immediately see to follow upon the former two. our present argument therefore, we will, if you please, state as follows: in consequence of this originate, self-derived and independent happiness of the divine being, and the having it in his power with the utmost ease and in the highest perfection to accomplish all his views and purposes, it is manifest that all those occasions and sources of evil dispositions that we know of towards other beings are excluded. " my dear
" children, you have, I dare say, so good
" an opinion of the rest of your fellow-
" creatures, as to imagine there is none of
" them that would do either you or any
" man any harm purely for the harm sake,

Lec. VIII.
⎱Argument *a priori.*

" or

Lec. VIII. " or were there not some temptation or
" seducement inclining him to it; or were
" it not for some preceding perverseness
" and corruptness of temper." rashness,
revenge, envy, ambition, pride, the love
of shining in the world, of exercising
power and appearing to be possessed of it,
care and the fretfulness it occasions, opposition of interests, inordinate desires, losses
and disappointments creating regret and dis-
gusts; these and the like are the sources of evil
dispositions and actions among men. nor do
we ever suppose any one to be malignant
by nature. even the devils became so out
of pride and envy; and were so far from
being originally malicious or evil in their
nature, that they were indeed as we know
in their first station the innocent, pure and
holy angels of God. and would it not be
very strange that the creator of the world
should be the only exception to this rule?
yet must this needs be the case if he be not
good. because none of those sources of
malevolence, which we just now mentioned,
can have any place with respect to the
deitie on account of his infinite power and
wisdom and independent happiness. the
deitie must either be a benevolent being, or
else

else malevolent and ill-designing. and if none of the several causes and sources of malevolence or ill-will which we can possibly conceive of, or imagine, can with respect to the deitie have any place at all; and if on the contrarie there be nothing that we know of which in like manner excludes the idea of goodness as an attribute belonging to his nature; this surely we are to ascribe to him. these however are considerations, which naturally tend to heighten and confirm our idea of this divine goodness; supposing it to have been already in the general proved, as in fact it has been, from the actual effects of it. for a self-existent being, that is continually and every where doing good, must needs be by nature good. now what is it that hinders the goodness of great numbers among our fellow-creatures, of which we are witnesses, from rising to an inconceivably higher degree than human goodness ever yet attained to, but one or another among those things, which have been mentioned as the sources of a malignant and evil disposition. hence those defects and blemishes that we observe even in the best of human characters. in some of which benevolence

and

Lec. VIII. and good-will would appear with a moſt aſtoniſhing luſtre, were it not for the oppoſition it meets with, the depreſſion it is ſubject to, and the impediments that lie in the way of it, ariſing from the evil tempers of others, and the diſturbances which theſe occaſion in their own breaſts. but every thing of this kind being abſolutely and of neceſſity excluded from our idea or notion of deitie, it being abſolutely impoſſible that any the leaſt impediment whatſoever ſhould interrupt the free, exuberant flow of divine benevolence, this naturally tends to give us the largeſt apprehenſions of its extenſiveneſs and permanencie. it is not unuſually obſerved that men are then moſt diſpoſed to communicate happineſs, when they are moſt of all eaſie, happie and contented in themſelves; and in the preceding reflexions we ſee ſome ground for an obſervation like this. God then muſt be infinitely and immutably good, becauſe he is infinitely happie.

Other But ſecondly, a very ſtrong argument may be drawn in proof of the divine goodneſs from that which is actually exiſting among other beings, in the ſame manner as we proved the divine power and the divine wiſdom,

wisdom, from the actual existence of power and wisdom as the qualities of other beings.
"I hope, my children, you have not forgot that argument. it was shewn, you know, that God must needs have more power than any one man, because every man's power is derived from him; and for the same reason he must have more power than the power of all mankind put together; and for the same reason still more than all the power of angels added to this intire sum or aggregate of human power, because of all angelic power as well as human, he alone is the source." in like manner it was argued with respect to the divine wisdom. nor can any thing more directly tend to fix and ascertain our ideas of the greatness of the divine power and of the extent of the divine wisdom, than the attending to and revolving in our minds some such reflexions as these. but now in the very same manner may the goodness of God be proved, not only to be a real attribute of his nature, but likewise to be inexpressibly large, free, copious, and in the highest degree perfect. "you, my dear children, I dare say, would do every thing that lies in your power to make
"another

Lec. VIII. "another being happie. and you have, I doubt not, the same opinion of your fellow-children, of your parents, and of vast numbers of your acquaintance." now, if all this goodness were, as it were, laid together, and supposed to constitute the temper and disposition of some one among mankind, and to it were added in order to constitute still the temper of some one being, the goodness of all the most sublimely generous souls that ever lived upon earth, the goodness of all the angels and hosts of heaven; in short, every degree of goodness from the highest to the lowest, that was ever possessed by any rational or moral agent whatsoever, would it not form a most amazingly perfect character of goodness; a goodness which could never be exhausted, never fail or disappoint our expectations? now nothing can be more evident than that the divine and sovereign being must be possessed of a degree of goodness beyond what this whole aggregate of love and benevolence would amount to; this whole sum of goodness belonging to all other natures whatsoever, being in fact derived from and communicated by him. for he is the author and giver " of every
" good

"*good* and perfect gift." the very quantity therefore or sum of goodness actually subsisting among other beings is a direct and of itself sufficient proof of his perfect goodness. and indeed what more naturally to be imagined, than that the supreme creator should make the rational and moral agents, which he produces, in the image of himself? if the devil, for instance, had it in his power to make other beings, where would be the wonder, if he should fill their hearts with spite and malice in his original formation of them? as God therefore in his creation "has written the contrary law "of love upon our hearts," we may from hence certainly conclude that his own moral nature is the direct contrary to that of malevolence, namely kind and gracious. even the inanimate creation bears the image of God's goodness by its universal tendencie to good, which would be altogether unaccountable, if the author of it were not good. but man is the still nearer and more exact image of deitie, by having the very disposition itself of goodness infused into his nature, and the "law of kindness" inscribed upon his heart.

Lec. VIII. But there is, thirdly, another thing remarkable in the conſtitution and frame of man, which ſeems ſtrongly to evince the goodneſs of his creator, and that is, that we are not only ſo formed as to be diſpoſed to do good ourſelves, and to be in our inclinations kind and benevolent, but likewiſe to love and admire goodneſs in others, and to hate its contrarie. now this is a ſtrong proof of the goodneſs of our creator in two different views. firſt, as it has ſo apparent and powerful a tendencie to the production of general happineſs, by encouraging goodneſs in others, and animating the temper in ourſelves. and then, ſecondly, if God were not good but the reverſe, and one or other he muſt be, he would, by this conſtitution of us, have made us with a diſpoſition to hate himſelf; which it is not ſurely to be imagined he would do. again, fourthly, in the moral order of things relative to mankind, it is obſervable that they are not only ſo conſtituted as to produce goodneſs and the love of goodneſs, but alſo to reward and honorably to diſtinguiſh it. "tho' the juſt and the unjuſt, "the unthankful, as well as the good," ſhare in the common mercies of providence,

Moral admiration.

Moral order.

yet

yet are the good in proportion to their goodness distinguished by peace of conscience, by reputation, by well ordered and prosperous affairs, (a) by lively expectations and animating prospects. now what can be more unlikely than that a being, who was not himself good, who did not love and delight in goodness, should so plan and regulate his own constitution of things, as that in the series and order of them this qualitie should be so perpetually rewarded in others? I here take it for granted that such is the constitution of man as we have now been representing it to be. the proof of these things will naturally come to be treated of in that other part of our intended series of discourse, of which man himself is to be the subject. and I think from all that has been said concerning his inward constitution and moral frame, from his bodily structure and organization, from the harmonie and friendly tendencie so visible

(a) Take this for a truth, to which oracles are fables; that never any man commits a sin to shun an inconvenience, but one way or other, soon or late, he plunges himself by that act into a far worse inconveniency than that he would decline. *Boyle* on *Customary Swearing*, p. 45.

Lec. VIII. and confpicuous in every part of the animal creation, "the heavens above, the earth beneath," and the waters of the mightie ocean, it muft needs be evident, that there cannot be any truth more clearly and firmly eftablifhed than this of the divine benevolence. and I have been the larger in treating upon this particular attribute of the deitie, not only on account of its tranfcendent moment and importance according to its own immediate nature, being the great center of all our hopes, that without which all the feeming lovelinefs of nature would be but rudenefs and deformitie; but likewife becaufe this being once clearly eftablifhed, the other moral attributes of the divine nature are proved of courfe, being indeed neceffarily involved in the true idea or notion of this; fo that it will be even altogether needlefs to produce any diftinct arguments in confirmation of them. nor indeed fhould we be able to produce any to this purpofe, but what would have their foundation in that goodnefs already proved, and be derived from the fuppofition of it. all therefore that we have here to do, is to fhew briefly, how it is that thefe other attributes do all of them flow out of this;

Moral attributes

in

con-

constituting as it were so many parts or branches of it. thus for example, if God be infinitely and immutably good, he must of necessitie be infinitely and immutably holy. " for I suppose, my good children, " your idea of holiness is this; that it " consists in the approbation and love of " goodness both in our own character and " in that of other beings, and in an an- " swerable dislike of its contrarie; an aver- " sion to every thing that would taint or " corrupt the moral character, and make it " to degenerate towards the temper of " malignitie or ill-will." the more firmly likewise the temper of goodness is established in any moral agent, and the less likelyhood there is of his ever deviating from it, so much the more holy do we esteem him. now on all these accounts, if God be an infinitely good and gracious being, it cannot but follow, that he is an infinitely pure and holy being. because we see that goodness among men in proportion to its prevalency in the mind and temper natuturally and unavoidably excites a love of and complacencie in the like character, wherever we behold it; an hatred of its contrarie, and a generous indignation at
the

Lec. VIII. the observed indulgence of malignitie and ill-will. " God therefore must, as you
" know, my dear children, the scripture
" expresses it, be a being, who is *of purer*
" *eyes than to behold iniquitie*, that is, with
" approbation, or otherwise than with the
" highest abhorrence and displeasure. and
" on the contrary he must be a being who
" *loves righteousness* and righteous persons.
" so that to all good people there is the
" greatest comfort to be derived from the
" consideration of the divine holiness, as
" we shall hereafter have occasion to shew
" you more particularly." and then lastly,
as nothing can be more evident, agreeably
to what has just now been insisted upon,
than that the more firmly any one is *rooted*
and grounded in love, so much the less likelihood there is of his ever deviating into
the contrary temper; that being who " is
" love" itself, pure and infinite love, and
the origin both of all that happiness and
of all that benevolence, that is any-where
existing throughout the whole scene of
nature, must needs be at an infinite remove
and distance from all moral depravation;
that is to say, he must be infinitely holy,
so that there cannot be a possibilitie of the

least

least deflection in his nature from what is purely and consummately good. (a) and then again, as to the justice of God, " if
" you are satisfyed and convinced, as my
" dear children I hope you are, that he
" is infinitely good, you may be very sure
" that his justice does not mean crueltie
" and revenge, or the punishing offenders
" with the utmost rigor and extremitie of
" power ; for all this is directly contrary
" to the plain, essential idea or notion of
" goodness. and therefore, if this were
" the meaning of God's justice, you would
" by ascribing it to him, deprive him of
" his goodness." but God is good as well as just; and therefore we are to form such a notion of his justice as is compatible and consistent with his goodness. nay, from his goodness we shall be certainly able to infer his justice according to the genuine and true idea of it. thus for instance, a good king that loves his subjects, will for that very reason, and because he is so, and for no other reason, take care that justice
shall

(a) " The holiness of God," Dr. Clarke defines to be " in general, that disposition of
" the divine nature, by which he is infinitely re-
" moved from all *moral evil whatsoever*." See his Sermons, Vol. II. Serm. VIII. p. 178.

Lec. VIII. shall be duly administered throughout his kingdom, and that wholsom laws shall be well and faithfully executed. in like manner the laws of God's moral government are calculated for the good of those who are the subjects of it, to which, in consequence of his goodness, he had a sole view in the original establishment of it. and for the same reason he will be just, that is, he will inviolably adhere to those laws in his continued government of the universe. they are calculated for the good of the universe. to depart from them therefore would not be goodness but the contrary. besides, mercie or forgiveness, " my good children, you
" know, is another attribute of the deitie.
" you must therefore needs form such an
" idea of the divine justice as shall be con-
" sistent with mercie, that is, with the
" forgiveness of offenders upon their re-
" pentance. and that mercie is indeed in
" this sense a real attribute of deitie, you
" cannot but be sensible must immediately
" follow from his goodness. you know
" very well, that the higher opinion you
" have of any one's goodness, the more
" certainly and joyfully you can depend
" upon receiving forgiveness from him, if
" ever

EXERCISES.

"ever you happen to offend him, upon
"fignifying a fuitable and juft concern for
"having done fo. you take it for granted
"that he muft be merciful and forgiving,
"becaufe you know him to be good. if
"then the divine being be fupremely and
"immutably good, he muft for that reafon
"alone, and you cannot want any other to
"be affigned, he muft, I fay, for that rea-
"fon alone be confidered as being in the
"higheft degree merciful and propitious."

And now from what has thus far been delivered concerning the feveral attributes of deitie, concerning his goodnefs itfelf, as well as in relation to the divine wifdom and power, " we fhall, I hope, my good chil-
"dren, be prepared for anfwering without
"any difficultie, thofe objections, which
"have fometimes been infifted upon in re-
"lation to this now mentioned moral attri-
"bute of his nature. you may perhaps
"be almoft ready to think that, if the
"goodnefs of God be fo plain and clear a
"point as has now by us been alleged, it
"muft needs be very ftrange that any ob-
"jections at all fhould ever have been
"made to the belief or fuppofition of it;
"and to imagine that fuch objections actu-
"ally

LEC. VIII.

Objections.

Lec. VIII. "ally advanced againſt the principle, muſt
"alone be ſufficient to ſhew, that it is not
"indeed ſo clear and evident as we have
"been ſaying. but you are to conſider that
"there is nothing ſo plain or evident but
"what may by ſome means or another
"come to be denied. and on the other
"hand it is obſerved by one that was him-
"ſelf famous for philoſophiſing, that there
"was never any thing ſo fooliſh or abſurd,
"which had not by ſome philoſopher or
"other been aſſerted. and in the preſent
"ſubject, what men of candid and modeſt
"diſpoſitions have at moſt conſidered only
"as difficulties, thoſe of more forward
"and preſumptuous ſpirits have formed
"into direct objections againſt this divine
"attribute. and it would increaſe their
"opinion ſtill of the force of theſe objec-
"tions, and diſpoſe them the more to tri-
"umph in this particular, were thoſe who
"aſſerted the divine goodneſs to decline
"the conſideration of them; nor is the
"conſequence at all to be feared. I am
"not for my own part, the leaſt appre-
"henſive of any force in theſe objections,
"that can at all impair the ſtrength of
"thoſe arguments that we have been ſo
"briefly

"briefly touching upon in proof of this great
"point. nay, I am not without hope of be-
"ing able to shew you, that the very things
"objected to are in realitie confirmations
"of the divine goodness, and not repug-
"nancies to the idea or notion of it."
however they may, I doubt not, be so obviated and cleared up, as to leave the mind intirely satisfied in the belief of it. but the discussion of these particulars, together with the inferences that are to be deduced from the consideration of this divine attribute, the duties founded upon it in its connexion with the other attributes of the divine nature, and the conclusion of this particular subject, we must refer to the next opportunitie.

LECTURE IX.

"KNOW, says the admirable Epictetus, that the principal point of religion consists in having right sentiments of the Gods. as for instance, to believe that they really are, that they govern the world with goodness and justice, that they are to be obeyed, that men ought to acquiesce in what they do, and indisputably follow their orders, as proceding from a most excellent and accomplished intelligence; for thus principled you will never charge them with ought, and you will not complain that they have deserted you." this, allowing only for that particular expression the Gods, which however was far from being meaned in this author in contrarietie to the notion of one supreme and eternal deitie, is language exceeding just and interesting. I therefore reflect with pleasure upon my having endevored in several of these our evening exercises, to establish your minds in a firm and rational belief of the divine goodness. by this means,

far

far from being terrified at the thought of the divine power, or having any formidable apprehensions of the wisdom, eternitie, omniprefence or immenfitie of deitie, or of his absolute knowlege of all hearts and of all events, you will be led to look upon all thefe divine attributes as being only the refidence and feat, or elfe the inftruments and agents of a benevolence that is infinite and unchangeable, and to triumph in them all, as affording you the firmeft fecuritie in conjunction with this amiably prefiding principle, that all the events of nature shall confpire to the moft happie and glorious refult; and that "no labor of love" in fulfilling the duties of life, or of patience in bearing the forrows of it, shall be without its ample reward from that God, "who "giveth to all men liberally and upbraid- "eth not." all that is farther wanting to complete our defign fo far as relates to this particular branch of our originally intended feries or order of difcourfe, is to confider on the one fide the objections that have been made to this doctrine of the divine good- nefs, and on the other the duties which naturally refult from our acknowlegement of it, as to the former of thefe particulars,

or

Lect. IX. or the objections that have been infifted upon to the prejudice and difparagement of this all-chearing doctrine, they have been founded partly upon the evils of the prefent life, and partly upon the apprehended torments of that which is to come. and there is ftill a farther divifion of thofe belonging to the former clafs, into the evil which is natural and that which is moral. the latter of thefe has been generally thought to carrie in it much the greateft difficultie with refpect to the reconcileablenefs of it to the perfection of the divine attributes. but for my own part I cannot fee the matter altogether in this light. miferie or natural evil has all the fame feeming repugnancie in it to the idea of benevolence as vice or moral evil has to holinefs or moral puritie, fo far as that is to be diftinguifhed from this very goodnefs itfelf. nay, the very turpitude and malignitie of fin itfelf confifts in its being a temper or difpofition of mind that alienates a man's affections from a juft concern for the happinefs of his fellow-men. fo that why an infinitely benevolent being fhould make a creature capable of falling into miferie, feems to be a queftion altogether as intricate as why

Evil.

an

an infinitely holy being should make a creature capable of sinning. nor can it be at all more difficult for the omnipotence and infinite wisdom of deitie to produce a preponderancie of good out of the sins of mankind, and to make them subserve the purposes of his own benevolence, than to do the same in relation to the calamities and afflictions which befall us.

And this leads me to mention it in the first place as a consideration that gives great relief to the mind under the apprehension of the ills of life, that from our natural conceptions concerning the greatness of the divine power, nothing can be more reasonable than to conclude, that those things which in the great affairs of divine providence carrie in them the most threatening and formidable aspect, and seemingly the most contrarie to the intentions of benevolence, may by that power be so controled and managed in relation to the consequences and effects of them, as even to subserve the designs of this very benevolence itself. the power of God is, as we have seen, a power exceeding all the united force and energie of nature, and of all the thinking active beings in the universe combined.

bined. it is a power therefore that muſt neceſſarily be able to govern and have under its management all theſe diſtinct and ſeparate energies. beſides, that all other power is in fact according to the purport of the proof alleged in ſupport of that other ſentiment, an effect produced by this. and the potter ſurely has " power " over his own clay." and God therefore for certain over his own creatures, ſo as to effectuate by their means whatever views his benevolence ſhall dictate. now what more eaſie than to conceive that by a power like this effects may be made to ariſe out of the ills of life, and ſuch a turn given to them, if I may ſo expreſs it, of which our own ſcantie and limited views can at preſent afford us no idea; but which may be altogether as pleaſing to us, when we come to diſcern it, as any of the moſt amiable and inviting appearances of nature whatſoever. we oftentimes do this or that, and when we begin to ſee what is likely to be the conſequence, ſay that, if we had thought of that, we would not have done ſo. and why, but becauſe it is not in our power to controle or ſet aſide this conſequence? but it is not thus in relation to the deitie. by the absolute perfection and plenitude of his power, he can with infinite ease prevent any of the natural evils of life from terminating in a greater quantitie of trouble and affliction to his creatures than he sees to be necessarie for their good. and whatever apparent or natural tendencie there may be in this or another vicious action of any of them, as in itself alone considered, towards the production of mischief and miserie upon the whole, he can by introducing other natural tendencies of a different kind, and that shall be of superior force, intirely prevent that mischief, and avert the threatening and apprehended ill. the like manner of reasoning is applicable in the second place to the wisdom of God. as by his power he can controle any event, so as that it shall in fact minister to the purposes and views of his own benevolence, how contrary soever may be its present aspect; so likewise his wisdom being complete and boundless, what wonder if in innumerable instances, where we can see nothing but calamitie and distress, he should be able most clearly and certainly to discern some highly beneficial purposes that may be served by the apparent ill? thus

I the

LECT. IX. the ingenious artificer out of a rude and shapeless mass of metal, in which another can see nothing but deformitie, and concerning which he might be apt to conclude that it can be good for little or nothing, can by the exertion of his skill and application of his art produce a most elegant and beautiful
Statuary. statue, which, for want of the like skill and abilities, we could never have effected, and which would be to the last degree surprizing and astonishing to one who had seen such a shapeless mass of metal, but had never seen or heard of a statue that had been produced from it. in like manner shall we hereafter be surprized by innumerable beauties, blessings and joys which we shall see to have arisen, in consequence of the mightie power and infinite wisdom of the deitie, out of what may now appear to us in the highest degree foreign to any such effect. (*a*) but this indeed I would chuse
to

(*a*) And here, though in a place less proper than I might have chosen, if I had timely remembered it, I shall both in reference to the extraordinary accidents that sometimes happen in *crises's*, and more generally to the seemingly irregular *phænomena* of the universe, venture to offer to you a notion, that perhaps you will not dislike.

to make a distinct observation upon the present topic, namely in the third place, that in the eternitie of God's duration we may find the highest satisfaction in relation to those various ills of life, which have been so much the theme and subject of com-

dislike. I think then that, when we consider the world and the physical changes that happen in it with reference to the divine wisdom and providence; the arguments for the *affirmative* ought, in their kind, to have more force than those for the *negative*. for it seems more allowable, to argue a providence from the exquisite structure and symmetry of the mundane bodies and the apt subordination and train of causes, than to infer from some physical *anomalies*, that things are not framed and administered by a wise author and rector. For the characters and impressions of wisdom that are conspicuous in the curious fabric and orderly train of things, can with no probability be referred to blind chance, but must be to a most intelligent and designing agent. whereas on the other hand, besides that the *anomalies* we speak of are incomparably fewer than those things which are regular and are produced in an orderly way; besides this, I say the divine maker of the universe being a most free agent, and having an intellect infinitely superior to ours, may in the production of seemingly irregular *phænomena*, have ends unknown to us, which even the *anomalies* may be very fit to compass. *Boyle*'s Inquiry into the Notion of *Nature*, p. 244, 245.

LECT. IX. complaint. the power, the wisdom, the goodness of God are all eternal. and surely in the eternal exercise of these attributes there must needs be room and opportunitie abundantly sufficient for educing the most happie consequences out of those various evils which are at present appearing, but which neverthelefs in comparison of eternitie are but of a moment's duration. *our light affliction*, as the apostle most excellently and charmingly observes, *our light affliction* whether arising out of what we call natural evils, or out of the evil actions of men and their mischievous intentions towards ourselves, *which is but for a moment, worketh for us a far more exceding and eternal weight of glorie.* " my good children, re-
" member this maxim, imbibe this truth,
" establish it in the *thought of your hearts*;
" and you will never think of repining
" against providence, or of looking upon
" any of its dealings towards you, as
" being any ways harsh or severe. for,
" can it think you be natural, can it be
" just or decent to insist upon a moment's
" pain as an objection against the good-
" ness of that God, who is designing you
" for an eternitie of happinefs, and who
                            " will

EXERCISES.

" will make even this momentarie pain
" contribute to the completion of that
" happinefs?" and then farther, fourthly, not only is God eternal, but his providence likewife as to the objects about which it is converfant, is immenfe and boundlefs in the extent of it. fo that in the objective fcene of divine government, as well as in the duration of it, there is room for a prodigious degree of preponderating good to take place and to arife even out of thofe very evils, that you or I may be complaining of. it is eafie for us to conceive, in general, tho' it be not eafie for us exactly and minutely to difcern at prefent, how that which we call our affliction may be operating to the good and happinefs of fome other beings. frequent inftances of this kind we actually fee; and from hence we may naturally conclude that there are others of the like fort in the great plan of providence, not as yet perceived by us. fo that the afflictions of life may have this double good in them, however grievous they may feem to us at prefent, that, whilft they are contributing to the final and everlafting happinefs of thofe who labor under them, they may be the means of no flight

LECT. IX. or inconsiderable blessing to those who do not. and thus you see that in all the other attributes of deitie there is abundant ground of consolation with respect to the evils of life, and that they all conspire in enabling us to reconcile with ease these evils to the perfection of his goodness.

But perhaps it may not be amiss to illustrate these reflexions by an instance or two in fact. " I doubt not, my good
" children, but you have read, and found
" it to be an high entertainment to you,
Joseph. " the historie of Joseph. you remember,
" to be sure, how his brethren envied him
" on account of his appearing to be hap-
" pier and more deserving than themselves,
" and they were resolved, if their own
" spite and ill-nature could effect it, to
" make him otherwise. they studied by
" all the means they could think of to pro-
" voke and incense, to plague and tor-
" ment him. and, as for poor Jacob his
" father, he was almost at his wits' end for
" the loss of this his son, whom he sup-
" posed to be dead. here was a scene of
" great crueltie, and seemingly very af-
" flictive and calamitous; and yet you
" remember how it turned out at last."

this

this very Joseph came afterwards by means of this very persecution to be a great man in Egypt. by which I do not mean only that he came to be in a very high station in the court of Pharoah, tho' that be true. but yet it is not high station alone that makes a great man. but Joseph was good and therefore great. he employed that influence which by this means he became possessed of for the good of others. and it is surprizing to reflect upon the innumerable good consequences which followed upon his being sold by his brethren. by means of it the whole land of Egypt was saved from a famine. and not only so, but his father Jacob and his family, and even his brethren, who thus evilly entreated him, were by this means supplied with the necessarie provisions of life. so that had it not been for this very event, of which amongst other unwelcome scenes the good old man so bitterly complained, saying, " all these things are against me," he and all his family must have been starved. and by this event likewise a way was made for his settlement with them in the land of Goshen, a part of Egypt, where they became a prosperous and a florishing people.

Lect. IX. among whom after their departure out of Egypt the true God was signally known and worshiped amidst the surrounding idolatrie of the heathen world. here then we have one most apparent and conspicuous instance of God's bringing good, a prodigious, amazing, inexpressible quantitie of good out of one single occurrence seemingly not a little calamitous, and actually proceding from a very high degree of real guilt and iniquitie. and why may it not be thus in the universal and everlasting government of God with respect to every evil event, and to all the calamities of human life? I might likewise mention to you another most eminent and striking illustration of this particular, and that is the crucifixion of our Lord

Jesus. Jesus Christ. could any thing ever excede or equal the malignitie of that spite and envy with which his enemies persecuted this meek and holy " lamb of God, in " whose mouth there was no guile?" could any thing be more enormously wicked, or have a greater appearance of calamitie in human affairs, than that he who was " holy, harmless, undefiled and separate " from sinners, and who was continually " doing good," should be cut off in the very prime

prime of life by the rage of his enemies, LECT. IX.
and put to death as if he had been the worſt
of malefactors? yet ſo great, ſo infinitely
great were the benefits and advantages to
ariſe from hence, all well and moſt exactly
known to the divine all-ſeeing mind, for
which reaſon the malice of theſe enemies
of our Lord was ſuffered by divine providence to take its own way; ſo great, I ſay,
were the benefits and bleſſings to ariſe from
this event, that our ſavior is ſaid in ſcripture to have been " delivered by the deter-
" minate counſel and fore-knowlege of
" God." it was by this very crucifixion
of the Lord of life, that he became the
ſavior of the world. and the very blood
their malice ſpilt was deſigned to waſh away
the ſins of the world, to be a propitiatorie,
atoning ſacrifice for them; and by this
means to be the ground and foundation of
eternal happineſs to all who in holie faith
and humble penitence applie its ſaving
benefits to themſelves. had it not been
for the ſhedding of this moſt precious blood
upon the croſs, there had been no ſuch
thing as the Chriſtian name or Chriſtian
religion now among mankind. with theſe
inſtances before our eyes, how can we think

I 5 any

LECT. IX. any longer of infifting upon the evils of life as objections to the goodnefs of God? have we not in confequences and effects like thefe, fome of the moft fignal and illuftrious proofs of it? " and indeed do you not
" obferve, my good children, what tem-
" pefts we fometimes have in fummer, and
" what fevere and pinching cold often-
" times in winter? I do, fir. but perhaps
" you may be ready to wifh that nought
" like this might happen; and that you
" were never more to feel the bluftering
" winds or piercing cold. " you would,
" however, my child, act very foolifhly
" and too much like a child in doing fo.
" for you know ftorms and tempefts, as I
" have already told you, cleanfe and puri-
" fie the air and prevent plagues, pefti-
" lence and death. and by the operations
" of a winter-feafon that vegetative power
" is communicated to the earth, without
" which the corn, notwithftanding all the
" invigorating beams of the fun, would
" never grow in fummer. now afflictions
" anfwer the very fame purpofes in the moral
" world, as do ftorms and tempefts and the
" blafting winter cold in the vifible and
" external fcene of nature. they are falu-
" tarie

" tarie and needful punishments and re-
" straints to the bad. they are fatherly
" chastisements and gracious discipline to
" the good. the scripture always speaks
" of them as being so intended: and thou-
" sands there are who have found them so
" to be. they are one natural means of
" promoting virtue and goodness, and con-
" sequently happiness; and therefore could
" not but have a part (*a*) in the plan of
" God's unerring and most gracious pro-
" vidence; as having an highly beneficial
" use and reference upon the whole, and
" being at the same time in themselves of
" a very transient nature. and they answer
" these ends in a manner altogether di-
" stinct, peculiar and wholly appropriate.
" never therefore look upon them as ob-
" jections to God's providence. you have
" a kind, indulgent father, it may be,
" who, as you yourselves are ready to ac-
" knowlege, is in all his actions consult-
" ing your good, excepting perhaps in one
" single instance or two of a discipline that
" may be somewhat severe, which you
" know

(*a*) See Discourses on the Parables of our blessed Savior and the Miracles of his holy Gospel, Vol. III. Serm. VIII. p. 189, 190.

Lect. IX. "know not at present how to account for, "and are at a loss how to reconcile to the "main and general bent of his conduct "towards you. would it not, think you, "be both very ungrateful and very absurd "in you to deny his goodness on account "of a single instance or two of seeming "severitie? and do you not rather still "believe him to be a perfectly good and "every way gracious father, and that he "has some good end to answer by this "severitie, which bye-and-bye you your- "self shall perceive? now all the evils "of this life are infinitely less in compari- "son with those lasting good effects, which "by the power and wisdom of the sove- "reign deitie they will be made to pro- "duce, than even the slightest imaginable "instance of severitie in a parent, who in "every other action you yourself would "confess appeared to your fullest satisfac- "tion gracious and benign. remember "eternitie, I say again, remember eternitie, "and you will not then suspect the good- "ness of your heavenly father."

And now as to the apprehended torments of the world to come; these likewise have been thought inconsistent with the good-

ness

ness of God. some would not have God to punish the wicked at all hereafter. but I am sure it would be no proof of his goodness not to do it; but rather of indifference at least to the happiness of his creatures, if not of a design to involve them in universal ruin. " should you, my child, think it
" any mark of goodness in king George,
" were he to open all those prisons, where
" so many of his wicked subjects are con-
" fined, and punished for their crimes, and
" give them the libertie to go where they
" would and do what they pleased; and
" then signifie by public proclamation,
" that for the future no man should be
" punished, let him commit never so many
" disorders; rob, steal, plunder and kill."
some future punishments then there must be, and very terrible they may prove without at all exceeding in degree what goodness itself will dictate. and this you may be sure will be the measure of them. God will punish hereafter as a being " who
" hates iniquitie." but he will punish too as a being " who remembers mercie, and
" whose compassions are infinite, who de-
" sireth not the death of a sinner, but had
" rather that he should return and live,
" who

Future punishments.

LECT. IX. " who would have all men to be saved and
" to come to the knowlege of the truth;
" and who can do all his pleasure." (a)

(a) *Justice* is the *justice* of *goodness*, and so cannot delight to punish; it aims at nothing more than the maintaining and promoting the *laws of goodness*, and hath always some *good* end before it, and therefore would never punish except some farther *good* were in view. Smith's Select Discourses, p. 153. and Plato in his Protagoras observes that no well-advised man ever punishes another for having done wickedly, but only that he may not do so for the time to come, and in order to prevent others from doing the like.—ἐ τῦ παρελυθότος ἕνεκα ἀδικήματος— ἀλλα τῦ μέλλοντος χάριν. Op. p. 288.

LECTURE X.

WE have been infifting of late upon the being, nature and attributes of God diftinctly. in particular we have treated at large and fomewhat copioufly upon his goodnefs, have pointed out the feveral clear and convincing proofs we have of it, have endevored to illuftrate, to explain and to enforce them; and to anfwer fuch objections as have been made to it. thefe are topics of infinitely higher importance than any other that can poffibly come under our inveftigation or review. religion is the nobleft fubject of human contemplation, and thefe are the nobleft fubjects in religion. " but yet, my good children,
" it is of the greateft importance for you
" to be informed and to remember it as
" long as you live; that it is not the
" higheft degree that you can in the beft
" ufe of your own reafon and exercife of
" your own judgment and underftanding
" attain to of knowlege in matters of religion, that will be fufficient for your obtaining the divine favor, which is to be
" the

Lect. X. "the grand and moſt earneſt deſire of your
"heart, it being not only that which alone
"can make you happie, but as it is like-
"wiſe your indiſpenſable and eſſential duty
"by chuſing God for your portion and
"your ſovereign good, to be aſcribing to
"him that honor which his perfections
"naturally demand from us. it is not,
"I muſt remind you, my dear children,
"even ſuch knowlege as this, however
"perfect in its kind, without your re-
"ducing it into practice, and making it
"the rule of your temper and guide of
"your life, that can conſtitute your
"happineſs, or put you in poſſeſſion of
"that trueſt and higheſt good, of which
"your nature is capable. to think rightly
"of God's goodneſs, to conceive of it as
"large, diffuſive, univerſal, boundleſs,
"unchangeable, everlaſting ; this is think-
"ing very honorably of him. theſe are at
"once the moſt lovely and the moſt accu-
"rate ſentiments that you can form con-
"cerning him. but ſtill he will not accept
"or be pleaſed with you on this account
"alone. for it is poſſible that you may
"have all theſe worthy apprehenſions of
"him, and yet be very negligent in reſpect
"to

EXERCISES.

" to that duty, which you are owing to — Lect. X.
" him. and if so, then the better thoughts
" you have of God, the greater must be
" your guilt in not acting this obedient
" part towards him. if a rebel were to — Rebel.
" acknowlege upon all occasions that his
" sovereign was a good and a gracious
" prince, that he himself had experienced
" his lenitie and kindness, and had long
" enjoyed the benefits of his protection
" and care, and had possessed many great
" and precious privileges under his auspi-
" cious reign, would not this, think you,
" greatly heighten and increase the guilt
" of his rebellion? just so it is in religion.
" to know God and to believe in him, ac-
" cording to the account or representation
" that has been laid before you in relation
" to his being and perfections, but yet to
" pay no regard to his precepts and laws,
" must needs be at once the most horrid
" guilt and the deepest miserie to beings of
" our rank and nature, capable as we are
" of paying a voluntary obedience to the
" great ruler of the world, and account-
" able for not doing so. you know and
" can recollect, I doubt not, what our
" savior says to his own disciples; *if ye*
　　　　　　　　　　" *know*

"know *these things, happie are ye if ye do
them.* now this plainly implies, that if
they did not do or practise *these things,*
their knowlege of them alone would not
suffice for their happiness. you will
therefore now, I hope, be glad to hear of
those duties which are owing from you
to that great and good being, who made
you and all mankind, and who continually supports both you and all your fellow-creatures in being, life and happiness. and be not discouraged at the
having such duties mentioned to you.
do not think that there are any hardships to be imposed upon you by religion. it is no pain or uneasiness to a good
and well-disposed child to be dutiful and
obedient to an indulgent parent; but on
the contrarie he finds it to be his highest
satisfaction and delight. and may you
not, think you, most safely and certainly
conclude from hence, that the service of
God can never be a burden to you? for
is he not your heavenly *father that has
made you?* and for this reason it is that
your dear savior has taught you in that
prayer of his, which I hope you often
repete with seriousness, and with a due

"con-

" consideration of God's knowing your
" thoughts, to say, *our father, who art in*
" *in heaven*; that by thus addressing your-
" selves to God under the title or appel-
" lation of father, you might be encou-
" raged to think that your obedience to
" him must needs be not an heavie, tire-
" some, tedious task, but a pleasant and
" delightful service; for no good father
" ever made his childrens dutie to be a
" burden to them. and from what you
" have already heard concerning the divine
" being, you see why it is that our savior
" teaches you to say *our* father, and not
" *my* father, namely, because God is not
" only your creator, preserver and bene-
" factor, but the maker likewise and pre-
" server of all; and *the lord, who is good*
" *to all, and whose tender mercies are over all*
" *his works*; and this is a sentiment which
" you should be highly pleased and de-
" lighted with, as well as with the thought
" of his being your own benefactor; other-
" ways you must come under the charge
" of having a narrow and selfish spirit.
" but by always thinking of God as being
" the kind and gracious father of all ra-
" tional beings, as well as your own, you
                                        " will

Lect. X.

Filial duty.

Lect. X.
Prayer.

"will be continually enlarging by degrees
"the benevolence of your own difpofition,
"and fo become more like God; you will
"come to look upon all mankind as your
"brethren, and by this means be induced
"to love them more heartily. and this is
"one of the duties which you owe to
"God; folemnly and ferioufly, frequent-
"ly, privately and publicly to pray to him
"as your heavenly father, and the creator
"and moft merciful preferver of all man-
"kind and of all rational beings. and
"this you are to do not with any imagi-
"nation, that the faying of fuch and fuch
"words, or the entertaining fuch and
"fuch thoughts in your minds, will of
"itfelf alone be any way available towards
"recommending you to the divine favor
"and love. but you are to do it in order
"to the having your own minds, (a) your
"hearts,

(a) Quicquid autem horum fit in orando ad *nos* pertinent non ad Deum. nec enim Deus delinitur audiendo laudes fuas, quemadmodum homines, fed nos laudantes illum magis ac magis elifcimus ac fufpicimus illius magnitudi- nem. commemorandis autem & exaggerandis malis noftris non hoc agitur ut *in diverfum mu- tatus oratione noftra* ex irato fiat *propitius*, fed ut *ipfi*,

" hearts, your affections impressed with a
" more lively sense of God's presence with
" you,

ipsi, dum melius magnitudinem nostræ calamitatis agnoscimus, vehementius expetamus illius misericordiam. itidem cum ea dicuntur, quæ pariunt attentionem, non hoc proficiscitur, ut Deus ante dormitans excitatur, cum illum nihil fugiat eorum quæ latent in cordibus hominum; sed ut nos instantius ac vehementius petamus, quod non promerentur recipere, nisi qui vehementer ambierint. Erasmi Modus Orandi, p. 123, 124. Dieu n'attend pas toûjours que les justes le prient: il leur donne souvent des secours qu'ils ne lui demandent pas; & s'il leur ordonne de les lui demander, c'est qu'il veut en être aimé & adoré. Dieu sçait mieux nos besoins que nous-mêmes; & s'il nous commande de le prier, c'est afin de nous obliger de penser à lui, & de le regarder comme celui qui seul est capable de nous combler de biens: c'est afin d'exciter nôtre amour vers lui; & non pas pour apprendre de nous ni nos besoins, ni les motifs qu'il a de nous secourir. il est resolu de nous faire grace à cause de son fils; & s'il veut que nous l'en prions au nom de son fils, c'est afin que nous l'aimions lui & son fils. c'est la foi & l'amour de Dieu qui prient: c'est la disposition de l'esprit & du cœur qui prie. on ne peut prier Dieu sans croire actuellement beaucoup des choses de lui & de nous; sans reconnoître sa propre foiblesse, sans esperer actuellement en Dieu, & sans l'aimer actuellement. mais les actes reveillent & produisent mêmes les habitudes.

Lect. X. " you, of your intire and absolute depend-
" ance upon him for *life and breath and*
" *all things*, and of his great and never-
" ceasing goodness to you. you are to do
" it that you may be the better able to
" take the comfort of such reflexions'as
" these when you come to meet with any
" of the afflictions and troubles of life,
" and that *in the multitude of your thoughts*
" *within you* on account of them these
" *consolations* may delight your souls; and
" that the thought of God and of his gra-
" ciously presiding providence may be so
" habitual to you, and so deeply rooted in
" your

tudes. c'est donc principalement pour reveiller en nous nôtre foi, nôtre esperance, & nôtre charité, & nous conserver dans l'humilité, que Dieu nous commande de le prier. *Conversations Chretiennes du Malebranche*, Entr. IV. p. 339, 340. and again, ibid. p. 341.—la priere est la nourriture de l'ame. c'est par elle qu'elle reçoit de nouvelles forces; c'est par elle qu'elle pense à Dieu, qu'elle se met en sa présence, qu'elle se unit à celui qui est toute sa force. ce'st même par elle qu'elle reçoit de Dieu par JESUS CHRIST la delectation de la grace pour contrebalancer les plaisirs prevenans qu'elle reçoit aussi de Dieu (car il n'y a que Dieu qui agisse en elle) mais qui sont involontaires & rebelles à cause de la desobéissance d'Adam.

"your minds, as that the peace and com-
"fort arising from it may be always at
"hand. and you are to do it, that by
"having such apprehensions as these of
"God always present to your mind, you
"may be the more fearful of sining against
"and offending him, and be more shocked
"at the thought of complying with any
"temptation to do so." but perhaps you
"will be ready to say; " I am, sir, very
"well satisfied in my apprehensions of the
"divine goodness. I firmly believe it;
"and am, I hope, better settled in my
"judgment upon that point by what you
"have been saying concerning it. but, pray
"sir, what expectations may I build upon it
"with respect to myself, and my own con-
"cerns and interests? this seems, sir, a
"point very necessarie to be determined
"in order to the regulation of my prayers.
"for how can I tell what I ought to make
"the matter of my prayer to God, if I
"know not what in reason I may expect
"from him? In answer to this question,
"my good children, I must tell you in the
"first place that you are not, because God
"is infinitely good, to imagine or to expect
"that he will do every thing for you that
                                   " you

*Expecta-
tions.*

"you may happen to defire." "why, fir,
"does not the pfalmift fay, that if *I delight
"myfelf in the lord,* which furely I do when
"I pray to him, if I pray aright, that he
"will *give me the defires of mine heart?*"
"indeed he does fay fo. but the meaning
"of that is, God is always ready to make
"you happie; and that is the *defire* of your
"heart; is it not? it is only for the fake
"of this fupreme and ultimate defire that
"you wifh for this or that particular en-
"joyment, fuppofing that it will contri-
"bute to your happinefs. but if in fact
"it is not likely to do fo, then I fuppofe
"you would rather be without it; and it
"would not be agreeable to the main and
"leading *defire of your heart,* which is hap-
"pinefs upon the whole, that it fhould be
"beftowed upon you. and yet in the wifh-
"ing for this or that particular enjoyment
"you may be often miftaken in thinking
"that it would make you happier by the
"poffeffion of it than you now are; and
"therefore it can be no way inconfiftent
"with the goodnefs of God to deny it to
"you. fo the fame pfalmift, as you re-
"member, fays, *the lord will give grace
"and glorie, and no good thing will he with-
   "bold

" hold from them that walk uprightly. but
" then, my dear child, you will, I sup-
" pose, be very ready to allow that God
" knows what is *good* for you better than
" you do yourself, and will be content
" therefore to leave it to him to judge for
" you. there are however many things
" which you may expect and certainly
" conclude that God will do for you, if
" you be careful to love and please him.
" thus in the first place, you may conclude
" from his goodness that he will bless your
" industrious and honest endevors in pro-
" viding for the things of this life, when
" you come to have that care upon you.
" not indeed if you mean by this the
" growing rich and great in the world;
" for that is not always a blessing. it is
" not necessarie to your happiness. many
" good men there have been in the world
" that have been extremely happy though
" very poor. but I mean that if you are
" not yourself *slothful in business*, but on
" the contrarie active and industrious, you
" will in the course of his providence be
" supplied with *food convenient for you*. and
" Agur, you know, prefered this not only
" to povertie but even to riches. *give me*
" *neither*

Lect. X.

Disappointments.

"*neither povertie nor riches*, was his prayer
"to God; and you cannot offer up in
"this refpect a better for yourfelf. in
"this or that particular defign too you
"may be difappointed, and yet God's
"bleffing attend your induftrie upon the
"whole in profpering and *eftablifhing the*
"*work of your hands*. even thefe very dif-
"appointments themfelves may contribute
"to it in the end, by making you more
"ferious, more patient, more circumfpect,
"and more indifferent to worldly good.
"and if you can be content with a little,
"that is altogether as good as having a
"great deal. fecondly, you may conclude
"from God's goodnefs, that he will not
"fuffer you to want any neceffarie direc-
"tion in the path of virtue; fo that if
"you are ignorant in this point, the fault
"muft be altogether your own. God has
"put the means of knowlege into your
"hands; that knowlege that is neceffarie
"to your falvation. *the word is nigh unto*
"*you*, it is in your heart, and it is in your
"bibles, and the more you confult it the
"wifer you will grow. and you may de-
"pend upon it that God will continually
"enlighten your minds more and more in
"the

"the knowlege of his truth, if you do but
"diligently apply yourselves to the search
"of it. *if thou searchest for her,* that is,
"wisdom, *as silver, and seekest for her as
"for hid treasures, then shalt thou understand
"the fear of the lord, and find the knowlege
"of God. for the lord,* it is added, *giveth
"wisdom.* this is the very reasoning
"which I have been pointing out to you.
"and I am glad that I can enforce it upon
"you by the authoritie of Solomon,
"whose, you know, are the words that
"have just now been recited. wisdom is
"the gift of God, from him it procedeth;
"and you may be sure that he is too good
"to denie it to any who sincerely seek
"after and desire it. again, thirdly, upon
"this head, you may be assured that God
"will fortifie you against the power of
"temptation so as not to suffer you to be
"overcome by it, unless you yourself are
"so careless as not to make a proper use of
"the gracious aids and influences he af-
"fords you. *he will not suffer you,* as the
"apostle expresses it, *to be tempted above
"what you are able, but will with the temp-
"tation also make a way to escape, that you
"may be able to bear it.* innocence and
"virtue

Lect. X. "virtue are necessarie to your happiness.
"and therefore you may certainly con-
"clude that God will never suffer you to
"lose the one, unless through your own
"remissness, or leave it out of your power
"even by your best endevors in resisting
"the force of temptation to obtain the
"other. and then in the fourth place,
"from the goodness of God you may na-
"turally conclude that he will not destroy
"your being, but that death will only be
"your removal into some other world,
"where you will see and discern that
"goodness much more clearly than now
"you do, and yourself experience much
"more of the effects of it, notwithstand-
"ing all the bright and glorious evidences of
"it that are even now presenting themselves
"to your view. for this life is very short,
"and the more you are convinced of the
"shortness of it, the less likely will it ap-
"pear to you that it should be the only
"period or scene of being alloted for us by
"so good and kind a creator, who can as
"easily continue our being in another
"world as he has preserved it in this.
"but, pray sir, what may I expect from
"the goodness of God in relation to
                            "others?

EXERCISES.

"others? for I cannot but interest myself
"in their happiness as well as mine own.
"why, you may expect in the first place,
"that he will continue to govern the whole
"world, as well as to direct the particular
"events of his providence that relate to
"yourself, in righteousness, and with the
"highest benignitie and kindness. and
"therefore when any public calamities
"happen, or some deep and dreadful dis-
"tress befalls whole nations and kingdoms
"at once, you may conclude that this is
"in mercie intended for the chastisement
"of a wicked people, and for the correc-
"tion of their depraved manners; and
"that if they repent, God will *turn away*
"*his anger from them that they perish not.*
"you may expect, secondly, that it *shall*
"*be well with the righteous,* and that they
"shall find happiness and peace, satisfac-
"tion and joy in pursuing the paths of
"virtue. this, as I have already hinted to
"you in your own case, may be very true,
"even tho' they should meet with many
"afflictions. numbers there have been,
"who, notwithstanding these have spoken
"highly of the goodness of God, have
"been very fervent in their acknowlege-

Divine judgments.

"ments

LECT. X. "ments and celebrations of it, have been
"very well satisfied with his dealings to-
"wards them, and very happie in the en-
"joyment of themselves. you may like-
"wise conclude, thirdly, from the good-
"nefs of God, that he will never suffer
"any of his human creatures to be misera-
"ble hereafter, except through their own
"wilfulnefs and folly; and that he will never
"oblige any man to be eternally damned by
"the power of his own decree. you your-
"self would never do such a cruel thing.
"you would detest and abhor the thought
"of it. and you may be sure that God
"is kinder than you. such then are the
"inferences which you may draw from
"God's goodnefs, and the expectations
"that you may ground upon it both in
"your own cafe, and in reference to the
"happinefs and good of others.

"But now let me, my dear child, re-
"mind you, that from the very account
"which I have been giving you of the
"nature and defign of prayer, you may
Other "infer that there are yet other duties
duties. "owing from you to the great lord and
"governor of the univerfe. and it is by
"the exercife of this that you are to be
"made

" made more sensible of, and attentive to
" them. I shall think myself, sir, very
" happy in having some brief account of
" them laid before me. well then, my
" dear child, in the first place, you must
" undoubtedly be under the highest obli-
" gations to love God, and to cherish in
" your heart the most fervent gratitude
" towards him. your own kind father
" upon earth you are thankful to, and
" think it your duty to be so, I doubt not,
" for the care he is continually taking of
" you, and the tenderness he daily ex-
" presses for you. and you would, I dare
" say, think it very base in you not to love
" him better than any man in the world.
" but now for the very same reason you ought
" to love God better than any being in the
" universe; that is, *with all your heart and*
" *soul, and might and strength,* because he
" surpasses all other beings in goodness and
" in goodness to you. but pray, sir,
" what is the difference between gratitude
" to God, and the loving of him ? for I
" observe that you mention these as distinct.
" why, to love God is to esteem and de-
" light in him on account of his goodness
" in general, the goodness of his nature,

K 4 " and

Lect. X. "and his benevolence to all his creatures.
" and gratitude is the loving him on ac-
" count of his goodnefs towards ourfelves.
" but fecondly, from what has been faid
" concerning the being and attributes of
" God, you muft needs perceive, my good
" children, that it cannot but be your
" dutie to refign yourfelves wholly and
" chearfully to his will ; and to the dif-
" penfations of his providence whatever
" they are or may be. for as he is not
" only fupremely good, but poffeffed of all
" power, and endued with unerring wif-
" dom, nothing can be more clear and evi-
" dent than that all he does, all the events
" of his providence and defigns of his uni-
" verfal government are for the higheft
" good of his creatures; fo that not to
" be refigned to his providence, and acqui-
" efcing in the difpofals of it, muft needs
" be in the higheft degree foolifh, pro-
" phane, and ungenerous. why foolifh?
" becaufe it is to be diffatisfyed with that
" which is beft for ourfelves. why pro-
" phane and impious? becaufe not to be
" pleafed with the meafures that are pur-
" fued by divine and infinite goodnefs,
" muft needs implie and carrie in it at beft
                                    " fome

" some defect in our love of that goodness.
" and why is it ungenerous? because it is
" repining at the dealings of that provi-
" dence which in all its dispensations has
" in view the common and most extensive
" good of the whole intelligent and moral
" creation. thirdly, you ought undoubt-
" edly to be very fearful of offending God
" by breaking any of his commandments.
" for to do so must needs be very ungrate-
" ful. and if you do in any instance trans-
" gress them, you may be very sure that he
" is acquainted with your disobedience
" and with the ingratitude of your hearts.
" and you know that in consequence of
" his own infinitely pure and holy nature
" he cannot but look upon every thing of
" this kind with the greatest abhorrence
" and displeasure. but then if you would
" discharge aright your dutie towards God,
" you must not only be fearful of offend-
" ing, but willing to obey him. this surely,
" as well as the other, is what gratitude
" must needs demand from you. we can-
" not be truly grateful to him, unless we
" are willing to obey him in every thing
" that he has signified to be his will or
" law with respect to our conduct and his

K 5 " injunc-

"injunction upon us. and whatever it
"be, and however reveled or made known,
"you may be assured that it is both for
"your own, and for the general good of
"all whom such a law or injunction may
"any way affect. and to refuse your obe-
"dience must needs be the height of inso-
"lence and prophaneness. not to obey
"with all possible chearfulness and alacri-
"tie, very inconsistent with those constant
"acknowlegements we are making of our
"perpetual obligations to the goodness of
"that sovereign being who commands it.
"again, it is our dutie to imitate God. if you
"ask me why? or should you be inclined
"to think that this is a dutie too high for
"your attainment; let me ask you, are
"you not capable of loving your fellow-
"creatures? now, to love them is to imi-
"tate God, who *is love*; and the more
"you love them, the more nearly do you
"resemble him in the high and infinite
"perfection of his nature; the transcend-
"ent excellencie of his moral character
"this you profess to admire, and to look
"upon as being in the highest degree ami-
"able. now observe, whatever in the con-
"duct and character of any of your fellow-
"crea-

"creatures you admire, and that you now
"think excellent and agreeable, you are
"defirous and fond of imitating it your-
"felf as far as you are able. and it is
"natural that you fhould be fo. for which
"reafon, by the way, you ought to be
"very careful what it is in this kind that
"you do admire. but to procede; if the
"reprefentation and reafoning that has
"now been infifted upon be juft, then
"certainly you muft be obliged to imitate
"God, becaufe you are obliged to love
"him. and if you do not defire to be
"like him, you may with too much reafon
"fufpect that you are far from loving him
"as you ought. and you may well believe
"that God cannot take any complacencie
"in thofe beings that are not like him,
"and yet are capable of being fo; for
"they are wilfully defective in that which
"is his chief delight; holinefs and good-
"nefs. and not to imitate his perfections
"is in effect to defpife them. how great
"and horrid an affront offered to the glo-
"rious majeftie of heaven and earth! but
"there is ftill another dutie mentioned in
"the holy fcriptures as what we are owing
"to the divine and fovereign being; and
"that

Lect. X. "that is the glorifying of him. and you
"may perhaps be still more surprized at
"the mention of this, than at that of re-
"sembling him. for how, you may be
"ready to ask, can we glorifie God?
"how! why can you not honor God?
"does not a *son honor his father?* now, to
"glorifie God is to honor him: and this
"you do in the most acceptable manner,
"by fulfilling the several duties that we
"have just now been speaking of. to love
"God, to submit to his will, to obey,
"and to imitate him, is most strictly and
"truly to honor him. you honor God
"likewise by being very desirous that all
"men should have honorable and worthy
"notions concerning him ; and by doing
"the utmost that lies in your power, and
"within the sphere of your acquaintance
"and influence, towards promoting such
"apprehensions of him in the world. in
"a word, you honor him by shewing in
"the whole course and tenor of your
"actions, that you are well pleased with
"being his creature, with your intire de-
"pendance upon him ; and that you are
"the subject of his moral government.
"and this is what the apostle means when
"he

"he says, that *whether we eat or drink, or* "*whatsoever we do, we are to do all to the* "*glorie of God.* by the general course and "constant tenor of our actions we are to "declare and shew forth to all the world, "that we think well and honorably of the "great creator of heaven and earth, and "believe him to be in his nature and pro- "vidence the most worthy object of our "highest affection, complacencie, and "esteem." and thus we have, by the blessing of heaven, gone thro' the first part of our design in this evening exercise, which was to discourse concerning God, his being, his nature, his attributes; his providence, its realitie, properties and extent. the subject which lies next before us is man; his origin, his nature, his connexions, the end of his creation, his happiness, his duty; or the particulars of that obedience of which we have just now been speaking as essentially owing from him to God his maker.

LEC-

LECTURE XI.

Lect. XI.

Self-acquaintance.

NEXT in importance to the knowlege of God, is that of ourselves. it is a duty that has been founded high in all antiquitie. and the precept enjoining it was supposed in an especial manner to have come down from heaven. it is a dutie which we owe more immediately to God. for man being the first and principal of his workmanship here upon earth, to contemplate ourselves, to know our own frame, to survey its wonders, to acquaint ourselves with its goodly order and exquisite contrivance, must certainly be such an instance of deference and respect paid to the works of the almightie, which we cannot be negligent of, or omit, without manifest contempt and impietie. to be curious in searching out the nature and œconomie of inferior beings, and to overlook ourselves, the noblest fabric of God here upon earth; what is it but in effect to deprive the supreme being of the honor that is *due to his name* on account of it? for how can we justly celebrate his praises as the creator of man,

EXERCISES.

man, if we know not the nature of man? [LECT. XI.] and on the other hand, were we but well acquainted with ourselves, there is no subject whatsoever within the compass of human knowlege, that could give stronger accent to our praises, or more elevate and enliven our songs of devotion. the studie of ourselves likewise is of the highest importance in order to the right discharge of the duties of social life, or those obligations which we lie under to one another. how should we know what these are but by acquainting ourselves with our own frame and make both outward and internal? the better we are acquainted with ourselves, the better of course shall we know our fellow-creatures. and the better we know them, the better shall we know how to behave towards them. this likewise is a dutie of the highest importance with respect to ourselves. we cannot discern wherein our own true happiness lies without understanding our own nature. that which is the happiness of a man must be mine and yours. to know therefore what kind of happiness man in general is made for, must be to understand our own highest good. and it is for want of being familiarly and
duly

Lect. XI. duly acquainted with our own necessities, and of distinguishing between those which are imaginarie and those which are real, those that relate only to the better accommodation of our present being, and those which are essential to the happiness of our natures, that we betray ourselves into endless vanitie, and become subject to perpetual disquietudes and disappointments. did we but know ourselves aright, the world and the things that happen in it could never make so many fatal impressions upon the mind as we are daily perceiving them to do, both with respect to ourselves and others. we should then know what things we might pursue with the greatest prospect of success; what things were least in our power, and what the most so; and how to regulate our aims and measures accordingly. now that which naturally presents itself first to our reflection concerning man, according to what has hitherto been so largely insisted upon, is that he is the creature of God. if there be any thing in this world that has derived its being from God, this must needs be equally true of man. for is he conscious to himself of any self-supporting power belonging to him more than

EXERCISES.

than to the meanest reptile? he "feels no "virtue of this kind going out of him." he stands in the closest connexion with other dependent beings, and must therefore needs look upon himself as ranking under that denomination too. he finds, he knows, that he cannot continue himself here in being one single moment. nor can he with all his own care, had he nothing else to depend upon, provide himself with any one necessarie article of life. he may procure seed to sow, and he may prepare the earth for its reception, and throw it in and cherish it; but what will all this effect without refreshing dews and rains, the ripening sun and vegetative power of the earth? over all which man has no more command than a worm. and even after he has eaten the bread that God has provided for him, does he not know that the digestion of it and distribution of its nourishing juices through the several parts of the body, and the circulation of its several different qualities into the corresponding receptacles, is a thing totally independent upon himself, and over which he has no power or command? "this, my good children, is what "the scriptures mean in saying that *man* "*liveth*

Lect. XI. "liveth not by bread alone, but by every word
"that procedeth out of the mouth of God.
"that is; it is not man's care alone in
"providing any of the conveniencies or
"accommodations of life for himself, but
"the divine blessing upon his industrie;
"not the bread which he eats by any in-
"dependent power or virtue of its own,
"but the continued agencie of a divine
"providence in the support and preserva-
"tion of its qualities, that is the true
"source and origin of life to man." can
we command the circulation of our own
blood? and yet how regularly does it flow?
this must needs be owing to some presiding
and directing mind. and as we are conscious that it is not our own, it must needs
be the divine, eternal mind; that sovereign
deitie, by whom we were not only at first
created, but are continually upheld and
supported in our existence. "you often
"talk, my good children, of such a one's
Relations. "relations, and of your own relations.
"and you know in general what the term
"imports. but it will be happy for you
"to extend your views both with respect
"to yourselves and to mankind in general
"as to this particular, according to what
"we

" we have juft now been faying. you see
" what an important *relation* there is fub-
" fifting between you and the fovereign,
" eternal deitie. he is your creator, your
" preferver, your benefactor, your friend.
" and as it is he only that has made you
" happie hitherto, fo it is he only that can
" accomplifh all your wifhes. this there-
" fore muft needs be the moft important of
" all your *connexions*; and one that you can-
" not be too frequently or ferioufly mind-
" ful of. and from this confideration, my
" good children, you will learn to be hum-
" ble." man is a very noble creature. he
has power, and he has reafon. he has wifdom, fkill and dexteritie. a fancy and imagination that can take prodigious flights,
expatiate at large in the region of ideas;
and form to itfelf a thoufand pleafing and
airie conceits. by means of thefe feveral
faculties he can wonderfully entertain both
himfelf and others, hit upon numerous inventions that may be of the greateft utilitie
both in the profecution of his own affairs
and with refpect to the concerns and interefts of others, cultivate the knowlege of
many noble fciences, acquire an high degree of facilitie in many curious and profitable

Lect. XI. fitable arts. and on all these accounts many of our species are apt to be not a little proud and arrogant, and to think highly, vainly and insolently of themselves, and very contemptibly of others, whom they imagine to be in any of these particulars their inferiors. " but, do you think, my
" good children, that there is in any of
" these endowments a sufficient reason for
" being proud? no, sir, I think from
" what you have been saying, it plainly-
" appears that there is not, because, how
" great and eminent soever may be my en-
" dowments and qualifications, I have
" received them all from God, and depend
" intirely and every moment upon him for
" the continuance and enjoyment of them.
" so that I cannot but apprehend that
" were my powers and faculties, and the
" several excellencies of my being a thou-
" sand times greater than they really are,
" I should still have no more reason to be
" proud than I have at present; because
" it would be equally true in relation to
" these more distinguishing and superior
" excellencies of nature, that I had re-
" ceived them from God, and was intirely
" dependent upon him for the preservation
" and

"and continued possession of them. you
"imagine then, I suppose, that there is
"no such being as a proud angel in hea-
"ven? I cannot but conclude so. must
"not pride then be to the last degree un-
"natural and insufferable in man? indeed,
"sir, I cannot but think it must. it is a
"matter of great consequence, my good
"children, in regard to your moral tem-
"per, to connect these things in some
"such manner as I have now been inti-
"mating, because I would by no means
"wish you to entertain a mean and grove-
"ling opinion of your own natures; but
"on the contrarie to think honorably of
"yourselves in this respect. because by
"this means you are more likely to think
"honorably of your maker, to be excited
"to noble aims and pursuits, and to look
"upon vice and wickedness as what would
"be a shame and disgrace to you; and to
"abhor every thing of this kind as wholly
"repugnant to the nature and constitution
"of your own minds. but then it is at
"the same time a matter of the greatest
"importance to you; to your usefulness,
"to your character in the world, to your
"own ease, quietness and self-satisfaction,
"with

Lect. XI. "with respect to the improvement of your
"mind in virtue, and to your acceptable-
"ness in the sight of God; that you be of
"an humble temper and disposition. and
"you see how easy a matter it is to recon-
Humilitie. "cile these two things; this humilitie of
"temper with an honorable opinion of
"your own natures, only by considering
"that you *have* nothing but what you have
"*received*, and that you are nothing with
"respect to the prerogatives of your being,
"but what God has made you to be. you
"see, in short, that an arch-angel has no
"more reason to be proud than a worm,
"because the former is as truly the crea-
"ture of God and dependent upon him
"for being as the latter. and this natu-
"rally suggests another particular in rela-
"tion to the nature and constitution of
"man, which amidst the high prerogatives
"and honors of your intellectual and moral
"frame may justly serve to keep you hum-
"ble. and you will, I hope, be gladly re-
"minded of it. What I mean is this;
"that, though by the intellectual and
"moral powers belonging to your natures,
"you are indeed allied even to the very
"angels of heaven, they being like you,
"reason-

" reasonable creatures and moral agents,
" only of a prodigiously higher class and
" order in this kind than man; yet by
" means of another part of your formation
" you are made to have something in com-
" mon likewise with the mere animals of
" the earth. you are like them dependent
" upon the fruits of the earth for suste-
" nance. you have a body like them,
" which stands in need of continual re-
" freshment and supply, and you are liable
" like them to bodily fatigue, and under
" the necessitie of bodily labor. and to
" your bodie and theirs there are many of
" the same materials belonging. when-
" ever therefore you are disposed to enter-
" tain any proud and arrogant conceit of
" yourself on account of your mental en-
" dowments, or the capacities and powers
" of your soul, or of the beautie of your
" outward form, which, whatever it be,
" however exquisite and captivating, you
" are wholly indebted to God for it; to
" God, who made you out of the dust of
" the earth, and framed the intire fabric
" of your bodie; you may very naturally
" check, restrain and bear down such fond
" and airy conceits, by reflecting upon
" this

Lect. XI. " this affinitie, that there is, great and
" exalted as you are on other accounts in
" rank and dignitie of nature, between
" you and the brute creation." this then
is the firſt truth that naturally prefents itfelf to our reflection concerning man, that
whatever be his endowments, whether as a
rational and moral being, or as an inhabitant of this inferior world, he is wholly
the dependant and the creature of God.
" you perceive, my good children, that in
" fpeaking of man as a rational creature,
" we have defcribed him as a being that is
" capable of forming a great many defigns,
" and of hiting upon various apt and well-
" adjufted means for the execution of
" them, of acquiring the knowlege of a
" great varietie of objects, of perceiving
" the differences and relations of things
" around him, and of difcovering a great
" number of truths in reference to them.
" but are there not, think you, fome me-
" thods of employing this general facultie
" much more excellent and important than
" others ; fome truths which by means of
" it are to be difcovered that are of much
" greater confequence with relation to his
" happinefs than others ? yes, fir, I cannot.
" but

EXERCISES.

" but apprehend that there muſt be a very
" great difference in this reſpect. what
" then do you ſuppoſe to be that kind of
" knowlege, or thoſe particular diſcoveries
" about which the reaſon of man was prin-
" cipally deſigned to be employed, and to
" which he may moſt honorably applie it?
" I apprehend, ſir, that it muſt be the diſco-
" verie and the knowlege of God, for which
" I find by what we have been ſo lately con-
" ſidering upon that head, man is by the
" reaſoning powers of his mind very natu-
" rally qualified. and as he is ſo, I muſt
" needs look upon this to be the higheſt
" and nobleſt exercife and object of his
" reaſon, and in all reſpects the moſt inte-
" reſting and important. you ſuppoſe it
" then to be the diſtinguiſhing honor of
" man as a reaſonable creature, that by
" being ſo he is fited for the knowlege of
" God (a). but did we not ſometimes in
" ſome

(a) Q. 8. *How muſt God's creation be* ſancti-
fied ? When we look on or think of the incom-
prehenſible glory of the ſun, its wonderful
greatneſs, motion, light and quickening heat,
of the multitude and magnitude of the glorious
ſtars, of the vaſt heavenly regions, the incom-
prehenſible, inviſible ſpirits or powers, that
actuate

LECT. XI. "some of our former conferences speak of man, not only as being a rational creature, but likewise as a being endued with moral powers, and as being constituted a moral agent; pray what is it that actuate and rule them all; when we come downward and think of the air and its inhabitants, and of this earth, a vast body to us, but as one inch or point in the whole creation; of the many nations, animals, plants of wonderful varietie, the terrible depths of the ocean and its numerous inhabitants, &c. all these must be to us but as the glass, which sheweth somewhat of the face of God, or as the letters of this great book, of which God is the sense; or as the actions of a living body, by which the invisible soul is known. and as we study arts for our corporal use, we must study the whole world, even the works of God, to this purposed use, that we may see, love, reverence and admire God in all: and this is the only true philosophy, astronomy, cosmography, &c. Q. 9. *What is the sin which is contrary to this?* Prophaneness; that is, using God's name as a common thing: and in this instance, to study philosophy, astronomy, or any science, or any creature whatsoever, only to know the thing itself, to delight our mind with the creature-knowlege, and to be able to talk as knowing men, or the better to serve our worldly ends, and not to know and glorifie God, is to prophane the works of God. and alas then how common is prophaneness in the world! Baxter's *Catechizing of Families*, c. xxv. p. 184, 185.

EXERCISES.

"that you suppose to be more distinctly
"meaned by this kind of language? I
"think, sir, I can separate in my imagi-
"nation the idea of knowing God from
"that of loving him, and worshiping,
"obeying and resembling him. and here,
"sir, I apprehend, lies the difference be-
"tween a rational and a moral creature.
"man as a rational creature is capable of
"knowing God; but it is only as a mo-
"rally constituted being that he is capable
"of loving and adoring him, and of sub-
"miting himself in the spirit of voluntarie
"obedience to his laws. you have made
"a very just and natural distinction. for
"the brute creatures can discern by their
"senses the outward objects of nature.
"but they can make no inferences, they
"can draw no conclusions from these ob-
"jects with reference to the existence of a
"creating mind as you can do; and are
"therefore not rational creatures as man
"is. in like manner we may suppose it to
"have been possible, that man might, as a
"reasonable creature, have had the power
"of discovering and knowing his maker,
"or of believing in God; but yet for
"want of moral powers, not have been
"capable

LECT. XI. "capable of loving him, or paying any act
"of adoration or obedience to him. our
"moral capacitie or conftitution then is
"an advance in the excellencie and prero-
"gatives of our nature, and what renders
"man a vaftly nobler and more important
"being, than if he had been merely ra-
"tional. but for what reafons, and upon
"what grounds do you fuppofe man to be
"not only a rational but likewife a mo-
"rally reflecting being ? I think, fir, I
"have been led very eafily, very clearly
"and very certainly to deduce this truth
"from what I remember you to have al-
"ready infifted upon in proving the being
"of a God, from the conftitution and
"frame of man, and by thofe home-ap-
"peals which you have fometimes made to
"mine own heart, and of which I could not
"but feel the force. upon thefe appeals I
"could not but find that there was a
"charm and a lovelinefs in goodnefs and
"in doing good, that was in the higheft
"degree attractive of my efteem and vene-
"ration, and that could not but confer the
"higheft honor upon thofe to whom fuch
"a character was belonging. now from
"hence I cannot but infer that fuch
"perfons

EXERCISES.

" persons must be the proper objects of
" my love and approbation, on account of
" their being possessed of so amiable a qua-
" litie. and from hence again, that God
" must needs be the just and most worthy
" object of my highest love, because he is a
" being of the highest goodness. I think
" likewise that I cannot but be bound to
" imitate in my own conduct that which
" I thus inwardly and naturally approve in
" another; and that therefore by this prin-
" ciple of *moral approbation* belonging to
" my frame, I must have been made and
" constituted under an obligation to do
" good myself, and to cultivate the princi-
" ple of kindness and benevolence in mine
" own heart, as well as to love goodness in
" another. and could you not think of
" urging something farther still by which
" to shew that you yourself, and the rest of
" mankind are beings made for the love
" and practice of moral virtue? yes, sir,
" I am apt to flatter myself that I can.
" will you let me know how you would
" procede? I perceive, sir, that besides
" my being inclined by nature to approve
" of and to admire benevolence and doing
" good, I have something within me that
" prompts

Lect. XI. " prompts me to be doing good myself,
" which leads me to take an instant plea-
" sure in performing an act of kindness to
" my neighbor, or in relieving his wants.
" I am shocked immediately, and without
" any farther reflection, and ere I can have
" time to recur in my thoughts to that
" *moral sense* (a) which we have just now
" been

(a) " There is ingrafted in the mind of man
" an intellectual *sense*, a discernment of what is
" good and evil ; as in the *eye* a sensible one of
" white and black ; in the *palate* a taste of
" bitter and sweet ; in the *ear* a power to dis-
" criminate harmonies and discords ; in *all* a
" sense of pleasure and pain. *what* is harmo-
" nious, equal, congruous, and consequently
" *pleasing* and agreeable unto practique reason,
" and accordingly approved by it, which it
" honours with a *dictate*, that it ought to be
" pursued or effected, that is called *morally*
" good ; and *what* is disharmonious, unequal
" and incongruous, and consequently *painful*
" and disagreeable, and accordingly disallow-
" ed, of which the understanding *dictates* that
" it ought to be *avoided*, that is *morally* evil.
" to be *morally* good or evil, is to be good or
" evil in point of *manners*; good and evil in
" manners are the *objects* of the *practique under-*
" *standing*; there are things agreeable or dis-
" agreeable to the mind and practique under-
" standing, as well as to " other" senses.
" there are things good and things evil to this
" high

"been speaking of, at the sight of miserie, and run to its relief. now, as I am endued with these benevolent and compassionate principles, instigating and prompting me to correspondent actions, and at the same time have *another* principle in my frame that disposes me to approve of them, I cannot I think but from hence infer that the very reason of my being endued with these principles, was, that I should cultivate and exert them, and that I should look upon it as my duty to do so. not to do it would be acting contrarie to the will of my maker discovered in my frame, and therefore im-

"high and racy sense, as well as to inferior ones." *Burthogge's* Apology, p. 398 – 400.
—Hyl.—" were that quicker *sense* revived in us whereby we discern moral good and evil, adultery, drunkenness, murther, fraud, extortion, perfidiousness, and the like; all these would have infinitely a worse scent to our souls, than this which you say is so stinkingly evil can have to our noses." *More's* Divine Dialogues, Vol. I. p. 285. " there is a *sense* in a man, if it were awakened, to which these *moral incongruities* are as harsh and displeasing, as any incongruous object, be it never so nauseous, is to the outward senses." *Ibid.* p. 286, 287.

" pietie.

"pietie. besides, I find myself so connected with mankind, and all mankind
with one another, that it is only by mutual offices of love and friendship that
societie or the body of mankind in general originally designed for happiness by
the creating deitie, can in peace and
comfort subsist. and by the universal
exchange of such offices all would
become extremely happy and be well
pleased with themselves and with their
condition here. and this, methinks, is
another consideration, that jointly with
what I have already ventured to mention,
strongly intimates what we were made
for, and points out the end of our being,
that which should be our aim in life;
the proper business and the natural duties
of it. and the evidence, I think, sir,
rises thus: I am so made and constituted
as to approve good actions. I am naturally prompted to the doing of them.
the exercise and practice of goodness is
necessary to the well-being of societie.
it effectually secures it. benevolence
therefore, love or goodness, must needs
be the law of our maker, and the naturally incumbent dutie of our situation
here."

" here. but among other things, which
" you find to be affirmed concerning
" man, you have no doubt heard him
" spoken of as being a social creature;
" what is the idea or notion that in your
" own mind you affix to that term or cha-
" racter given of him? it seems, sir, in a
" great measure to coincide or to express
" the same sense with that character of
" him already discussed, or the moral prin-
" ciples belonging to his frame and nature.
" he is a social creature, because he is by
" his nature fited for and obliged to social
" as well as religious duties; the love of
" man as well as the love of God; doing
" good himself, as well as admiring good-
" ness in another; and exerting himself in
" behalf of his fellow-creatures, as well as
" praying for them to God. besides, he
" is a social being on this account, that
" he is made to take pleasure and satis-
" faction in the company of others, and in
" discourse and conversation with them.
" but I observe you speak of benevolence
" only and love, as being the duties of
" man considered strictly as a moral agent,
" and by way of distinction from his reli-
" gious character and relation. are there
" no

"no other duties incumbent upon you as
"a moral agent, or as a subject of God's
"moral government, even according to
"this more limited idea of it? do you not
"think that man is bound likewise to be
"temperate and juſt, and to be true to his
"word and promiſes, and to the truſt re-
"poſed in him? o ſir, I am fully con-
"vinced that he is ſo. but then I appre-
"hend that all theſe will follow of courſe
"from that of love, or are comprehended
"in it. ſo that by proving that to be his
"dutie, I do by neceſſary conſequence
"prove theſe likewiſe to be incumbent
"upon him. why, my dear child, this
"ſeems to be a very comprehenſive and
"compendious method indeed of aſcer-
"taining the ſeveral duties of moralitie
"which you have hit upon. but pray how
"will you make it good? indeed, ſir, I think
"nothing can be plainer than that if a man
"be obliged to do all the good he can in
"the world, he muſt neceſſarily be obliged
"to preſerve himſelf in the beſt capacitie
"for exerting the powers and abilities be-
"longing to him in ſuch a view; and this
"can only be by being *temperate in all*
"*things*. if I am obliged to contribute
"all

" all I can to the welfare and happiness of
" another, I muſt needs be under an equal
" obligation at leaſt not to do him any
" wrong; and that is to be juſt. if I am
" to aim at promoting the peace and wel-
" fare of mankind, I muſt needs be bound
" to purſue this aim by methods that are
" moſt likely to anſwer ſuch an end, and to
" make me in fact uſeful to others. and
" this ſeems to me, ſir, to be the ſame
" with prudence. and as by breaking my
" word, violating my promiſe, or betray-
" ing my truſt, I manifeſtly do an injurie,
" I can neither be juſt nor benevolent, if
" I allow myſelf in any ſuch practices.
" but are there not ſome of your fellow-
" creatures whoſe welfare you are more
" obliged to conſult than that of others?
" I imagine, ſir, that there are. and who
" are they? my benefactors. and why ſo?
" becauſe gratitude does in this caſe con-
" cur with the general law of benevolence
" to excite and inſtigate my kind and lov-
" ing affection towards them; and the cir-
" culation of friendly offices is greatly pro-
" moted and encouraged by the return of
" one good action for another. and are
" there no others to whom you are obliged
" in

Lect. XI. "in a peculiar manner to be kind and
"friendly? yes, fir; those of my own
"kindred and family. and why? because,
"generally speaking, these are our greatest
"benefactors; and providence has placed
"me in a closer and more intimate con-
"nexion with them, which is a plain sig-
"nification given to me that I am to con-
"sult their happiness in the first place."
and the general interest of societie would
greatly suffer, if those to whom we
are most nearly and closely allied had
not the chief and principal share in our
kind and generous affections in pre-
ference to any equal number of other
individuals. and it would be worse for
all in general, if these were not by each
one in particular more especially to be
regarded in our acts of kindness and
love. "but I suppose you may sometimes
"likewise have heard it said of man that

Free being. "he is a free being. o! yes, fir, very
"often. and what do you suppose to be
"meaned by that expression? I imagine,
"fir, it is intended to denote that he is a
"voluntary and designing agent, capable
"of acting from his own choice, and not
"by constraint merely; with a meaning
"and

" and an aim, and not blindly and by rote
" only, or by the guidance and direction
" of another folely, like a machine; and
" that he has a power of chufing or re-
" fufing, as things appear to him. he is
" likewife I fuppofe called a free being,
" becaufe, of the right that he has to
" govern his own actions, and not be the
" flave of any of his fellow-creatures; to
" enjoy his own propertie without mo-
" leftation, and to exercife his own reafon
" and judgment in matters of religion
" without controle." (a) fo then it appears

(a) It is a man's *felf-governing* reafon and will which caufeth him to obey another: nor can a child perform any act of proper obedience differing from a brute's, unlefs by a felf-governing *act*. but parents government is the next to felf-government, and the government of hufbands, princes, and mafters, which are by contract, is next to that. every fubject therefore being firft a fubject of God, and next a felf-governor, is to obey as a reafonable creature, and to underftand what is his duty, and what not; and becaufe all is our duty which God commandeth, but not all that man commandeth, God's power being abfolute, and all mens limited, therefore we have nothing to do with the laws of God but to know them, and *love them*, and *obey them*. But as to man's commands, we muft know alfo that they are not
con-

LECT. XI. pears that man is by his nature a derived, dependant, rational being, made for the know-

contrary to God's laws, and that they belong to the office of the commander. If a parent or prince command you to blaspheme God, or worship idols, or deny Christ, or renounce heaven, or not to pray, &c. you must obey God by disobeying him. and if a king command you not to obey your parents, or will chuse for you your wife, your diet, your physick, the words you shall say to God in your secret prayers, &c. these are things which belong not to his office, no more than to a captain's to become judge of the Common Pleas. Baxter's *Catechizing of Families*, c. xxxviii. p. 292, 293. *Wo unto the world because of offences!* for what an abominable and horrible sin is it for a man to give occasion to others of falling into [this] sinful fear, and thereby to hinder their conversion? but yet this is not sufficient to excuse those, who fear man more than the living God. would to God the magistrates might here open their eyes to see the *sad effects* of their overforwardness in determining and regulating divine matters, by which they very much obstruct the edification of others, and pinch it within such narrow bounds, by tying it up to their manner and form, though no such limitations are to be found in the word of God, and bind the consciences of men, where God has not bound them, and take upon them the judgment which God has reserved to himself! true it is, that by this means they make themselves to be feared

EXERCISES.

knowlege of God, and a moral agent, con- Lect. XI.
ſtituted the ſubject of God's moral government, fited and deſigned for the exerciſe
both of religious and of ſocial duties, and
for the pleaſures ariſing hence, endued
with a libertie of directing his own actions
and of forming a judgment for himſelf in
all matters of inquirie and ſpeculation, and
for the preſent actuating or animating a
bodie. ſuch his rank and nature. of his
actual condition and character here on
earth, and of his hopes and expectations,
in our next.

feared by men, and are an occaſion of turning
aſide many that were in a fair way to repent-
ance, to diſſimulation and hypocriſie. but they
will once to their great ſorrow be made ſenſible
who they be that are concerned in that of our
lord; *wo unto them that ſhall offend one of theſe
little ones.* See a ſtriking treatiſe, intitled *Nico-
demus*, by *Aug. Herman. Franck.* p. 26, 27.

LECTURE XII.

Lect. XII. WE have already, and upon the laſt occaſion of this kind, treated of the nature of man, and conſidered him according to the ſeveral properties and characteriſtics of it as he is a derived, dependant, rational being, made for the knowlege of God, and as a moral agent conſtituted the ſubject of God's moral government, fited for the exerciſe both of religious and ſocial duties, as likewiſe for the enjoyment of religious, moral, and ſocial pleaſures; endued with a libertie of directing his own views and actions, and of forming his own judgment in all matters of inquirie and inveſtigation, and for the preſent connected with and animating a body. we are now next to treat of his actual condition and character here on earth, and of his hopes and expectations reſpecting futuritie. many

Hope   hopes and expectations in relation to the " life that now is," we have entertained and cheriſhed in our minds after a very ſanguine manner; have built much upon them, and formed to ourſelves an imaginarie

ſcene

EXERCISES.

scene of most exquisite satisfaction and delight to be enjoyed, when we should come to be in possession of the object of these hopes. but alas we have found them disappointed! either we have never attained the desired good, or if so, we have found it to be only a fancied one: nay, that we have by means of it been betrayed into much vexation and mischief. such in many instances at least has been the case with respect to the hopes and expectations that we have hitherto entertained, and which one way or another we " have seen an end " of." and such may be the case with respect to a thousand more of the like kind that we may be now entertaining and cherishing in our breasts, or may hereafter indulge. and yet is not this owing so much to the uncertaintie of our present situation or the precarious issue of human affairs as to the irregularitie and vanitie of our own affections in fixing upon those objects which we make to be the matter of our hope and eager expectation. were we but in this respect a little wiser, we might hope even in relation to the matters of this present life with much greater probabilitie, and with no small success. thus the husbandman

LECT XII.

Differing kinds of.

LECT. XII. bandman plows and sows, not indeed with the certainty or absolute assurance of a crop, but yet with the rational expectation of it. and for the most part throughout all the different regions of the world he finds his expectations gratified and answered. and thus has it been for a long succession of years, and in the general course and order of this world's affairs. though the gratification may at some seasons perhaps have been a little delayed, and some circumstances of a discouraging nature, and that seemed to bear a contrary aspect, may have intervened. and in any other rational and honest pursuit industriously applied to, we may in like manner entertain the hope of having our labor recompensed with the desired success. thus we find in general that those who undertake the care of a family with the hope of providing for it, and exert themselves in a proper manner for that purpose, rarely fail of meeting with that success, which if they be moderate and regular in their views, may abundantly content and satisfie them. there are then with respect to the things of the present life, hopes or expectations of two different kinds. such as are vain, romantic, visionary and fruit-

fruitlefs, and thofe other that being founded upon probable grounds and well confidered reafons, and upon the natural appearances, order and ftate of things, are generally accomplifhed. and it is thefe latter, I prefume, that will be found to be the true emblem or model of thofe expectations which we are all with fo much fatisfaction and joy entertaining in relation to a future exiftence, in which we fhall be far more happie, infinitely more exalted in dignitie and bleffednefs, than any thing that by any means we can attain to here can enable us to conceive of; and that this hope is of the folid and rational kind, not chimerical and vifionarie. and if with refpect to fo great a varietie of other things we may hope with reafon and fuccefs, why not in this ? " St.
" James, as perhaps, my good children, you
" may remember, inftances in that very
" cafe of the hufbandman, which we have
" juft now been fpecifying, to the very
" fame purpofe, and as being the natural
" emblem of human hope and expectation
" with refpect to a future ftate. *be patient,*
" he fays, *therefore brethren.* and it is a
" paffage, which as you grow up you may
" have frequent occafion of meditating
" upon,

LECT. XII. "upon, and may find great comfort and satisfaction to arise from the revolving of it in your thoughts. *be patient therefore brethren unto the coming of the lord. behold the husbandman waiteth for the precious fruit of the earth, and hath long patience for it, until he receive the early and latter rain. be ye also patient; stablish your hearts. for the coming of the lord draweth nigh.*" thus it is that he speaks concerning our hope of blessedness hereafter, as being altogether as rationally founded as that which is entertained by the honest, industrious and skilful husbandman of a plentiful crop. but before we enter more directly upon our proposed illustration of this particular, we are to consider, according to the method that has been intimated, of the present actual condition of mankind. and we shall briefly touch under this head, upon his external, his religious, and his moral condition or state. as to the first of these, it has often been observed that those of the

Infant state. human species come into the world in a much more infirm and helpless state than is the case with respect to many of the mere animal class; so that for a considerable time after our birth we are wholly unable either

either to provide for ourselves, or to be of any service to others. and yet upon the whole it is very evident that the infant condition of man is so far from being worse than the situation and state of the mere animal tribe when newly entered upon their lower state of being, that it is in all respects incomparably more eligible. what may seem to be defective in the helpless condition of the infant, is abundantly made up by the tenderness, reason and wisdom of the parent. so that helpless as we then are in ourselves, there is in the gracious order of a divine and heavenly providence, an ample provision made for our being nourished and brought up. and by that intire dependance which we have upon our parents in this our infant-season of life, and that care and tenderness, which during the period of it, if not perfect monsters indeed, (*a*) they do not

(*a*) Nothing can more strongly or beautifully point out the realitie and force of this principle than the application made of it by the supreme being in the language of his prophet, in order to illustrate the infinite compassion and mercifulness of his own eternal nature. *Isaiah* xlix. 15. " Can a woman forget her sucking
" child, that she should not have compassion of
" the son of her womb? yea, they may forget,
" yet will I not forget thee."

fail to exercise towards us, the bond of mutual love, of gratitude and social affection, is rendered much more firm and solid for the future. and thus the most valuable purposes of a social kind are, by this particular dispensation or œconomy of providence, accomplished. a foundation is laid for a long and most lasting friendship between the parents themselves and their offspring in after-life, and for the delightful returns of gratitude on the part of the children, when parents in their turn come to stand in need of the filial assistance. and the social affections thus strengthened in this one particular instance, are by this means naturally improved into the more extended, the universal habit of goodness, and fited for exerting themselves after a more operative and effectual manner in other connexions, and in every varying scene of human life. " you, my children, are to remember as " you grow up, what prodigiously strong " and forcible obligations you lie under to " your parents on account of that perpe- " tual, unwearied care and tenderness " which they have shewn towards you in " your infant state, and to which alone, " under the divine blessing, you are indebted

" for

" for having got beyond it. had it not
" been for this you muft have perifhed in
" your infancie, and never have enjoyed
" the *light of life*, or had the pleafure of
" finding yourfelves gradually advancing
" towards manhood, and of being qualified
" by degrees for manly relifhes, and for
" engaging in fuch manly occupations as
" are belonging to the prefent fcene of
" things. often think, my dear children,
" through how many anxious days and
" months your parents denied themfelves
" of almoft every comfort and enjoyment,
" fubmited to almoft perpetual confine-
" ment, toil, wearinefs, fatigue, hazard,
" dangers, pains and forrows for your
" fakes. and all this, though you could
" never have done them any kindnefs be-
" forehand, and when they were altogether
" uncertain whether you would ever live
" to repay thefe *labors of love*, or whether
" if you did live to have the opportunitie
" of doing fo, you would have the inclina-
" tion. all this they did for you, though
" not knowing but poffibly you might,
" notwithftanding all their own beft ende-
" vors to prevent it, be through your bafe
" and wicked temper their future plague
" and

LECT. XII. "and burden. I hope, however, that this
"will not be the case with respect to any

Filial
"of you; and that you will so reflect upon
"what I have been saying concerning the
"tenderness of your parents towards you
"in your infant state, as never to think
"any thing too much to be done for them
"in grateful return; that you will wil-
"lingly obey all their commands; that
"you will chearfully endure any burden
"yourselves for the sake of lightening
"theirs; that you will reverence and love
"them, and have all possible tenderness
"for their interest and welfare, if ever
"they should come to want your assistance.
"all this is due from you. and how sadly
"unnatural and perverse will be your dis-
"position, if instead of this grateful re-
"turn you should slight and despise your
"parents, put them to all manner of in-
"convenience and trouble, and fill their

Duty.
"hearts with inexpressible pain and sorrow
"by your imprudent, or by your extrava-
"gant and untoward conduct! *the eye that*
"*mocketh at his father, and despiseth to obey*
"*his mother; the ravens of the valley shall*
"*pluck it out, and the young eagles shall eat it.*
"is not this very terrible? but you may
"be

" be ready to think that there have been LECT. XII.
" many undutiful children, whose *eyes*
" have never been *plucked out* by a *raven*,
" or *eaten* by an *eagle*. and that is very
" true. but let me tell you that Solo-
" mon's intention in this manner of speak-
" ing was not to intimate that this very
" thing itself would exactly and literally
" happen to disobedient and undutiful
" children, but by these sensible ideas to
" strengthen your apprehension of some-
" thing yet more terrible that must befall
" you, if this should be your temper and
" disposition. what a shocking terrible
" thing does it appear to you for any to
" have their eyes *plucked out* by one animal
" and *eaten* up by another. now, says
" Solomon to you, children, let me inform
" you, and be sure to remember it, that
" either that, or something which you will
" find to be still more shocking and terrible,
" must needs be your lot, if you behave
" with contempt, ingratitude and disobe-
" dience towards your parents. this is an
" unnatural, wicked, and dreadfully dege-
" nerate temper. it must therefore be
" highly displeasing to God, and bring
" upon you his indignation and wrath;
                        M   " and

Lect. XII. "and if perfifted in, cannot but terminate in the moft tremendous woe." but as our infant ftate is thus helplefs and infirm, the proper improvement of which, and the wife defign of providence in it, I have now been endevoring briefly to point out, fo likewife in our future life on earth we are expofed to a great varietie of calamities and forrows. "there is a time to laugh," it is true. but we all know that there is likewife " a time to weep." we form projects. but as we have feen, unlefs it be with great caution, wifdom and forefight, we are liable to no fmall difappointment in the event and iffue of them. and fometimes, even though ever fo prudently planned, vexation and difappointment does neverthelefs attend them. many evils are we thus liable to fuffer in confequence of our own imprudence, or elfe of our neceffarie and unavoidable defect in wifdom. and many more are we expofed to in confequence of the follie or injuftice of others. pain, ficknefs and diftemper of body attend us in one degree or another throughout the whole of life. or if we ourfelves be well, " our " friend Lazarus," it may be, " is fick." thofe, whofe company, health, profperitie and

and happiness is our own greatest joy, are laboring perhaps under many pains and infirmities of body, or if not under these, under worldly losses and disappointments of various kinds. in our own affairs of this nature we are liable, not only in many instances to the frustration of our hopes, but even to very urgent, pressing difficulties and embarrassments; so that we know not which way to look for, or whence, according to any outward means or human probabilities, to expect our succour. in the midst of all, however, providence has put into our power a great varietie of enjoyments by which life is or may be for the most part sweetened and made comfortable to us. there is a strength and fortitude naturally belonging to the mind of man, which may render evils tolerable; especially when it is aided and assisted by reason and reflection, by prudence and the moderation of our desires. several observations with respect to these ills of life, considered as objections insisted upon by some against the providence of God, have been already laid before you. but let me here both in farther answer to such objections, and likewise for your direction as to the manner of

Lect.XII. bearing these evils, and for your comfort and satisfaction under them, remind you as follows; that by such afflictions we are naturally put upon serious thought and recollection, that they have a direct tendencie to excite the due exertion of our rational faculties, and to a consideration of the true nature of human happiness. and by this means they produce upon the whole, a good far over-balancing their own pressure and weight of evil. by these disappointments and sorrows we are naturally put upon seeking our comfort in religion, and led to place our repose, our confidence and happiness in God. and is it not well worth our while to endure any ills of life for the sake of being brought to the devout and fervent love of God at last? or even of having the heavenly flame of devotion by means of them increased and heightened. and in a thoughtful, serious, well-tempered mind somewhat of this kind will assuredly arise out of the suffering scene, and be the effect of our afflictions. they will bring us nearer to God. they will be the means of uniting us more closely to him; and will thus be contributing to our truest felicitie and highest good. when we have made
God

God our " refuge and our hiding place," we are at once safe from storms, and in a situation for enjoying the most sublime and exquisite felicities. " God, we are then " enabled to say, is my portion; I will " not fear what man can do unto me." many of the afflictions of life are in a manner annihilated and made to vanish into a thing of nought by the power of religion. and others of them that may remain, it enables us with ease to bear; according to that admirable advice and exhortation of the psalmist, " wait on the " lord and be of good courage, and he " shall strengthen thine heart. wait, I " say, on the lord." and then farther in the third place, the various calamities of human life are furnishing us with perpetual occasions, and supplying mankind with constant opportunities, for the exercise of the social affections, the tender and sympathising passions. and by this means the highest good is effected; we are formed into the temper of virtue; we are made like to God; we are made fit for heaven; and by the few transient scenes of calamitie and sorrow here occuring, ripened for an everlasting world, where there will be no such

LECT. XII. such thing. the afflictions of others give
the opportunitie for exercising our kindness and good-will; and by our own we are made more sensible of theirs, and consequently become more disposed to embrace that opportunitie. thus do the evils of our external condition naturally tend to make us thoughtful, rational, manly in our views, sedate in our temper, religious in our affections, tender and sympathising in our dispositions towards mankind. happie fruits! most desirable end and issue of them!

Religion. But alas! when we come to examine secondly, the religious state and condition of mankind, we are far from finding these fruits universally to arise out of them: and in this the actual state and condition of mankind with respect to religion, we shall see the reason why they do not. though as we have seen, man is a being naturally formed for the knowlege and contemplation of God; yet how few are there who employ their thoughts or exercise their reason in this way? and yet so highly natural is religion to mankind, that they will have the appearance of it in one shape or another. and from this natural tendencie of the human mind to religion, in conjunction with

with so sad a neglect of employing our reasonable powers aright in the contemplation and study of religious truths and principles, have arisen those superstitions that have been so mightily prevalent in the world, and the cause of so many dire and horrid mischiefs among mankind. many have been tempted dishonestly to give their countenance to these superstitions; even though they themselves were well enough convinced of the follie and vanitie of them. thus there has been so much the less probabilitie of their being removed out of the way. and in the mean time those, who with greater innocence have embraced these false notions concerning deitie and religion, have had their tempers at once corrupted and disturbed by them. for it is not every thing that men may call religion that can afford us the comforts of it, but only true religion itself; religion in its own genuine principles and nature. we may call those principles the truths and doctrines of religion, which are directly contrarie to the real system of religion; and if so, can it at all be wondered at that they should have contrarie effects? that they should not produce the same? and then a great many others

LECT. XII. others there are, who never think about religion at all; who call it all superstition; who despise it in every shape and form; and who are so strangely infatuated, as to value themselves not a little upon daring to do this. " of this, my good children,
" you will see sad and melancholy instances
" when you come to look about you in the
" world, and observe the conduct of man-
" kind. but I hope you will ever remem-
" ber, that to despise religion, is in effect
" to despise God your maker, whose nature
" and perfections are the foundation and
" object of it. and glad, exceeding glad,
" shall I be, if what in these our evening
" exercises I have been saying to you
" concerning God, his goodness and his
" love to you, and his power to make you
" either happie or miserable, shall have
" made such an impression upon your
" minds, as that you will ever look upon
" it as the most odious, the most ungrate-
" ful, the most absurd and foolish dispo-
" sition that can possibly be indulged, to
" be indifferent to the sentiments of reli-
" gion; indifferent whether we love God
" or not; whether he approves of us or
" not; or even whether there be a God or
" not.

EXERCISES.

" not. I am sure the wiser and better you
" are, so much the greater horror will you
" have of such a temper." is it not sad
and grievous that, whilst God is ever so
intimately nigh to us by his supporting
and all-sustaining presence, by the acts of
his power, in the wonders of his love, yet
we should in temper and affection be almost
intirely estranged from him! who can reflect without a pious indignation, that it
should be the language of any human creature to God his maker; " depart from
" me; I desire not the knowlege of thy
" ways; who art thou, that I should
" serve thee?" and yet what vast numbers
are there amongst mankind, with respect
to whose temper and actions this language
expresses the apparent meaning and import
of them, though there be something in it
too horrid even for themselves to avow in
words? a circumstance of itself alone sufficient to convince them of their folly, if
they were not indeed almost hardened beyond conviction. but such is the religious
state and condition of mankind. we are
naturally capable of religion and disposed
to it; but yet through vanitie, levitie, in-
consideration, and the power of corrupt

Lect. XII. example, sadly unmindful of it. " the ox
" knoweth his owner, and the afs his
" mafter's crib." but we " forget the
" God who formed us, and lightly efteem
" the rock of our falvation." " but yet,
" my good children, there is a great deal
" of religion to be feen in the world,
" which you are to confider as the public
" teftimonie of mankind given in favor
" of it, and which fhould excite your cu-
" riofitie to enquire into the nature and
" meaning of it. you fee your parents
" and others, the whole neighbourhood,
" the whole citie, and you prefume the
" fame of the whole country and kingdom,
" affembling themfelves together upon the
" ftated days of public devotion. now by
" thefe actions God' is folemnly acknow-
" leged as the creator and ruler of the
" world. and you may very naturally
" imagine that mankind all over the world
" could fcarce have agreed fo unanimoufly
" as they do in fuch a practice as this, if
" there had not been fome very obvious
" and convincing proofs of God's being
" and government, which you to be fure,
" as well as many others, who have lived
" before you, may be very fenfible of, if
" you

"you will but seriously apply your minds to seeking of God your maker, "who giveth songs in the night." "*who giveth songs in the night*; you may be ready to ask perhaps, what is the meaning of that? why, it means the joy and comfort, which God gives to those of mankind, who humbly wait upon, and devoutly adore him in their afflictions." "songs" are a token of joy. and "the night" is a gloomy season; and is therefore a proper emblem of affliction; so that to "give songs in the night" is to give comfort in affliction.

<small>Lect. XII.</small>

The moral state of the world is much the same as the religious state of it. man is made for virtue as well as religion; which are indeed in the true and genuine idea of them very closely and inseparably connected; but he sadly neglects the one as well as the other. and yet so powerful are the tendencies of nature to both, that he cannot wholly overlook either the one or the other. "when therefore you, "my children, come to look abroad in "the world, if you do it with a candid "eye and after a friendly good-natured "manner, you will see a great deal of "generositie and kindness, of gratitude,

<small>Morals.</small>

"meek-

LECT. XII. "meekness, patience and forgiveness among
"mankind; which you yourselves must
"be desirous to imitate in your own tem-
"per, and to cherish in the minds of others.
"but yet you will perceive that there is
"not any thing like so much of these in the
"conduct and dispositions of human kind
"as might naturally be expected, and as
"would in fact take place, were we but as
"mindful as we ought to be either of God
"or of our own natures. and in many
"instances you will see most sad and la-
"mentable departures from a spirit of this
"kind. and, if the sight and observation
"of these do but increase your own indig-
"nation against vice and wickedness, it
"will be well and happy for you. and
"from what we have thus far been insist-
"ing upon concerning the external, the
"religious and the moral condition of
"mankind, you will easily collect what
"notion is to be formed of human happi-
"ness as enjoyed here upon earth; that
"the present is far from being a state of
"perfect felicitie; that yet there is a great
"deal of satisfaction and comfort enjoyed
"by mankind on earth; that there might
"be a great deal more, were they but more
                            "thought-

EXERCISES.

" thoughtful, and more attentive to religi-
" ous interests and concerns, and the cul-
" tivation of virtue and the moral temper;
" and that all the true and solid happiness
" that is enjoyed amongst us is owing to
" such a spirit: and that therefore, if you
" would either be happy yourselves, or
" make others so, you must live piously
" and delight in goodness yourselves, and
" endevor so far as your influence may
" reach to persuade others to the love and
" pursuit of pietie, and to the cultivation
" of the same friendly and benevolent
" dispositions." thus have we considered the nature of man and his present condition. that glorious interesting topic, his hopes in relation to futuritie, and the accomplishment of them in the blessed world above, must be reserved for the next opportunitie we shall have of meeting upon this occasion.

LECTURE XIII.

WHEN we treated laft in thefe our evening exercifes upon the great, all-important, univerfally interefting and infinitely momentous topic of religion, it was obferved that human hope had for its object both the good things of the prefent life, and the great realities and events, pleafures and enjoyments of a future ftate of being. with relation to the former, we then took notice that there are too very different ways or methods according to which our hopes are entertained and very commonly cherifhed by mankind, fo as to render them under one of thefe claffes or arrangements altogether chimerical and vifionary, and which are therefore for the moft part difappointed; whereas thofe belonging to the other being rational and upon fair and probable grounds affumed and taken up, come generally to be gratified in the end. how happy would it be for us, did we but confine ourfelves as much as poffible to thefe latter! and thefe, it was then obferved, would, as we prefumed, be found

the

EXERCISES.

the proper emblem of that other hope, in *Lec. XIII.* which we are so much more nearly concerned, than in any thing that can befall us here; that hope or expectation I mean, *Future state,* which we all of us with so much joy embrace of living hereafter in the world of spirits, and of entering ere long upon it. an hope, which looks " into that which is *arguments* " within the veil," which penetrates beyond the utmost bounds of time, and which gives us the chearing, triumphant prospect of being placed so soon in a situation, where no calamities can any longer annoy us, where we shall be for ever enjoying the happie fruits of those we now bemoan, and under which we ourselves are actually laboring, as well as be acquainted with the many beneficial consequences in that blessed world arising out of those, which others are now enduring, and we ourselves so oft behold with a lamenting and sympathetic eye. that this hope, so glorious, so animating, is indeed of the kind I have hinted, or, in other words, an hope founded upon the most solid and convincing arguments; arguments, which the most inquisitive and searching mind may with the utmost satisfaction relie upon, is what I am now to *in proof of.* shew.

Lec. XIII. shew. indeed, to us, who are favored with the *lively*, infallible *oracles* of christian truth, there is the most ample and decisive attestation given upon this head by the authoritie itself of these *lively oracles*, and in the express, frequent and most solemnly repeted assurances of our blessed savior and his holy apostles, to whom " God has borne witness " by signs and wonders, and divers miracles " and gifts of the Holie Ghost. by them " life and immortalitie" have been in a most glorious sense " brought to light." and upon this foundation we may with the utmost safety rejoice in the firm persuasion of being one day admitted to see the glorie of God as manifested and made known in the now inconceivable and inexpressible felicities, objects, employments and entertainments of the heavenly state. " but had you, my " dear children, the expectation of becom- " ing possessed ere long of some fair and " ample fortune in this world, by which " you were to be much raised above your " present rank, and even above many of " those, whom you now look upon, though " I hope without any envy, as your supe- " riors in this particular, would it be at all " displeasing to you to have this hope con- " firmed

" firmed by a varietie and number of wit-
" neſſes, who ſhould all agree in giving
" you the ſtrongeſt reaſons for entertain-
" ing it, and believing that it would in
" a little time be gratified and accom-
" pliſhed? would you not hearken to *each*
" of them? would you think that what
" any one had to ſay to you on this head
" was at all ſuperfluous, becauſe you knew
" of *another*, who could likewiſe give you
" ſatisfaction in relation to it? would you
" not on the contrary rejoice in the varietie
" of the evidence as greatly corroborating
" and ſtrengthening your hope? but how
" much more pleaſed ſhould you be with
" ſeeing this increaſe of evidence in relation
" to your hope of a future world? there
" will ſoon be an end to the higheſt honors
" of the preſent life, and, in a little time,
" the largeſt treaſure of worldly riches,
" that you can by any means acquire, will
" periſh and decay, or, which is all one,
" you yourſelves will be taken from the
" poſſeſſion of them; but if you are once
" entered upon the happineſs of futuritie,
" you will find it to be as complete in its
" nature, ſo likewiſe endleſs in its duration.
" I hope therefore it will be a great plea-
                                    " ſure

Lec. XIII. "sure and satisfaction to you to hear of
"having the realitie of this future happi-
"ness proved by the *light of nature,* and by
"arguments and reasons deduced from the
"innate and well-grounded suggestions of
"our own minds:" that is to say, by
such arguments as we might have made
use of, and been acquainted with and seen
the force of them, even though we had
never had any knowlege of Jesus Christ,
or of the declarations of his gospel. the
proving of it in this way will by no means
weaken or invalidate, or any way derogate
from that clear and certain proof of this
article that is to be drawn from the authoritie of his religion ; but will be just so
much additional strength to our evidence
and proof upon the whole in relation to
this so interesting and joyful a speculation.
we will therefore go on, if you please, to
enquire a little into this subject according
to the manner we have now been speaking
of. and in doing this we will endevor,
first, to point out the realitie of a future
state ; secondly, consider somewhat of the
nature of those rewards and punishments
that will be distributed in it ; and then,
thirdly, enumerate some of those inferences
which

which are to be made, and which we may naturally found upon this principle or doctrine. as to the firſt of theſe particulars, the realitie of a future ſtate of rewards and puniſhments, it is to be proved, firſt, from the nature and perfections of God; his goodneſs, his holineſs, his power and his wiſdom. ſecondly, from the inward frame and ſtructure, the mental paſſions and affections of man himſelf. thirdly, from his condition here, or the conduct of divine providence towards him in the preſent ſtate. theſe are the three grand and general ſources of argument upon this ſo highly momentous topic, ſo far as we can carrie our reflexions upon it, without having recourſe to the ſpecial illuminations and miraculous teſtimonie of the goſpel. upon each of theſe then I will now briefly inſiſt. there is ſomething very pleaſing in the following deſcription of the nature, power and efficacie of religion, which has been given us by Doctor Lucas in his inquirie after happineſs. " religion, ſays he, rectifies our " opinions and diſpells our errors, and " routs thoſe armies of imaginarie evils, " which terrifie and torment the world " much more than ſpirits and ghoſts do.
" this

CATECHETICAL

Lec. XIII. "this discovers to us objects worthy of all
"the love and admiration of our souls.
"this expiates our guilt and extinguishes
"our fear. this shews us the happiness
"of our present condition, and opens to
"us a glorious prospect of our future one.
"this discovers to us the happie tendencie
"of temporal evils, and the glorious re-
"ward of them; and, in one word, teaches
"us both to enjoy and suffer. - it moderates
"our desires of things uncertain and out
"of our power, and fixes them upon those
"things, for which we can be responsible.
"it raises the mind, clears the reason;
"and finally forms us into such an united,
"settled and compacted state of strength,
"that neither the judgement is easily
"shaken, nor the affections hurried by
"any violent transport or emotion."
"you see, my good children, how much
"the truth and proprietie of this descrip-
"tion depends upon that doctrine of a
"future state, which you perceive to be
"refered to in it." who then would not
wish to have all these glorious effects of religion ascertained and made to be reasonable
in the expectation of them, by the fullest
establishment and clearest proof of that doctrine?

trine? let us procede then to inquire what evidence in favor of it is to be derived from those several and distinct topics or sources of argument that have just now been mentioned, to wit, in the first place, from the nature and perfections of God, his goodness, his holiness, his power and his wisdom. this is an argument, the intire force of which cannot be comprehended but in a comparative view, and as connected with that which is to follow, and which is founded upon the nature and constitution of man. however some separate observations may usefully be made relatively to each of them; after which their united force shall be briefly pointed out. from the idea which we are naturally led to form of the absolute and unlimited power of the deitie, we may plainly and evidently collect that our existence hereafter must at least fall within the possibilities of nature. "you, my children, "will easily perceive that it must needs be "altogether as easy for the supreme being "to continue your existence in another "world as it is to support it now, or as it "was originally to bring you into being. "you can do one thing and not another; "nay, the very same thing you can do at
"one

Lec. XIII.

Divine attributes.

Lec. XIII. "one time and not at another. and why? "becaufe there are impediments and ob- "ftructions lying in your way, proceding "from fome other acting power in nature, "and which impediments it is wholly be- "yond your abilitie to remove. but you "will immediately perceive from what has "in the courfe of thefe exercifes been laid "before you, that nothing of this kind "can happen or take place with refpect to "the intentions and will of the deitie. if "the divine being wills your exiftence "hereafter, there is none, no man, no "angel, no devil, no inhabitant of any "world whatfoever, that can *ftay his hand*, "*or fay unto him what doeft thou*. fo that as "to the idea or poffibilitie of the thing, it "is altogether as eafy for you to conceive "that you may exift in another world, as "that you may be alive to-morrow in this. "and this let me obferve to you, is no in- "confiderable point in an argument of fo "much confequence; that the thing, "which we would prove is in the notion "or idea of it, of as eafy comprehenfion "as any of thofe familiar views or objects, "which you are every day converfant "with. you will not at all wonder to
"find

" find yourselves alive to-morrow, though
" you ought to be very thankful for it to
" that God, *in whose hands your breath is,*
" *and whose are all your ways,* and to whom
" alone you will be indebted for this far-
" ther extension of your being. many
" children, as well as persons of riper years,
" are very suddenly cut off by death, and
" whenever it seems fit and proper to sove-
" reign wisdom that it should be so. but
" I say, you would not at all wonder, my
" good child, to find yourself alive to-mor-
" row. now it ought not in reason to be
" any greater matter of surprize to you,
" that you are to live hereafter or in an-
" other world. *for with the lord a thousand*
" *years is as one day, and one day as a thousand*
" *years.* and surely, my dear children,
" when you recollect what has been so
" largely said to you concerning the good-
" ness of God, nothing, I imagine, could
" appear to you more natural, than the
" supposing that his goodness, so free, so
" disinterested, so large, so exuberant as it
" appears in fact to be from the surround-
" ing works of nature, and in the perpe-
" tual operations of his providence, should
" incline him to continue your being
 " beyond

Lec. XIII. "beyond the short and scanty limits of
"this world. the higher opinion you
"have of any earthly friend, of your own
"father, for instance, or mother, the
"firmer persuasion you have that they will
"continue to be as kind to you hereafter
"as they are at present; and that far from
"being disposed to deprive you of any
"good which you enjoy, they will be ra-
"ther inclined to multiplie the comforts
"of your being, and to enlarge and height-
"en the happiness of it. why then should
"you ever suspect that a being, who is
"infinite in goodness, should be so far
"from continuing to be good to you after
"death, as at this destined hour to deprive
"you even of that grand blessing, which is
"the foundation of all besides, your very
"existence itself? that after so very short
"a period, he should cease to have any
"kindness for you at all; nay, that he
"should then act the very cruellest part
"towards you that can possibly be ima-
"gined, next to the making you eternally
"miserable; namely, the striking you out
"of being for ever. upon these plain and
"obvious principles it must needs, I think,
"appear, that the higher notions you have
"of

EXERCISES.

"of the divine goodnefs, fo much the lefs _{Lec. XIII.}
"able you will be to fuppofe that God
"fhould deprive you of your being after a
"few years only paffed here upon earth,
"and the more readily will you conclude
"another ftate to be ordained for man."
when we mentioned the holinefs of God in
the ftating of this argument, we did it to
fhew, that if there be a future ftate at all,
it muft needs be a ftate of happinefs and
reward to the good, and of punifhment and
miferie to the wicked. and this is a truth
that you will eafily perceive muft neceffarily
and directly flow from that acknowleged
attribute of the deitie. for being that
righteous lord and fovereign ruler who *loveth
righteoufnefs*, and confequently righteous
perfons, nothing can be more abfurd than
to imagine that a future ftate fhould be to
any fuch a ftate of miferie and torment.
and it would be equally abfurd to imagine
that to any of thofe who enter upon it with
depraved and wicked difpofitions, it fhould
be a ftate of blifs. for God cannot "take
"pleafure in iniquitie." yet what could
be a greater evidence of his doing fo, than
the admiffion of the wicked and ungodly
into a ftate of perfect, heavenly and everlafting

lasting felicitie? this is the highest possible token that can be given of the divine love, even to the best and most virtuous of mankind. it is therefore a manifestation of it that cannot surely be extended alike to the wicked and prophane. nor would it be at all consistent with the wisdom of God, another attribute which we mentioned as comprehended in this first topic of argument, and in the general scope of it, that vice and wickedness should be thus triumphant hereafter. this would be giving it so much countenance as would be utterly inconsistent with the essential holiness of the divine being, and consequently with the nature and design of his moral government. but secondly, the realitie of a future state may be very strongly infered from the nature of man himself; from his inward make and structure, his mental powers and affections. man is a noble creature. he stands eminent and superior in rank of being; foremost and chief among all the works of God below. and a most prodigious difference there is between him and any of the brute creation. those of them that make the most superb and stately appearance in the animal tribe itself, what are

[margin: Human]

are they when compared with man, who is made capable of religion and virtue, of knowing and worshiping God, and even of powers, resembling his perfections? and in contemplations exercises and attainments of this kind he is naturally qualified for making a perpetual progress, far beyond what the narrow limits of this world will admit of, even supposing his religious and moral improvements to be carried on at ever so great a rate; nay, the more any man knows, and the longer he lives in the pursuit of knowlege, the more he perceives himself capable of knowing, the more eager he is after still farther knowlege, and the more exquisitely delightful he finds the pursuit and acquisition of it to be to him, and he cannot but apprehend that it will be continually more and more delightful to him the longer he continues to be so employed and in this manner entertained. the same observations are applicable to his religious and moral character. the more he loves God, the more he perceives himself capable of advancing in this divine affection, the more he desires to do it, and the greater idea he forms of the happiness that will result from going on to perfection in these

Lec. XIII. these devout aspirations of the mind. the more he delights in virtue, in imitating God, and doing good, the more raised and elevated are his ideas of the happiness to flow out of such a temper yet farther cultivated and improved, from the continued incessant progress of it, and from a farther extended series of such godlike action. this then being the case, this total, absolute, and in a manner infinite, disparitie considered between man and any of the brute creation in their original powers and capacities of being, is it at all probable, can we possibly imagine, that they should be alike in death? or can any thing on the other hand be more probable or more naturally apprehended, than that there should here too be an answerable disparitie? or what can be more incongruous to our notions of the divine wisdom, than to imagine that man should be thus nobly distinguished by the powers of his being from the brutal tribe, and yet with respect to the continuance of it be altogether upon a level with them? that he should be endowed with powers capable of being exercised and improved in a future and nobler scene of action and enjoyment, and yet his being

being be wholly confined to this? upon such a suppofition, what adequate end can we perceive to be anfwered by his being thus nobly endowed? "let it then, my
"dear children, be deeply impreffed upon
"your minds, that you are beings made
"capable of religion and virtue; and that
"it is thefe which conftitute even the hap-
"pinefs of heaven itfelf, and of all the
"glorious angels and arch-angels who
"there inhabit; and you will, I am per-
"fuaded, apprehend it to be much more
"probable, that you fhould be defigned to
"live ere long in company with thefe glo-
"rious beings and in that bleffed world,
"and in purfuing with an everlafting
"ardor the perfection of thefe your noble
"faculties, than that you fhould lofe your
"being like the *brutes that perifh*." from the nature of any work or fabric contrived by human art, we make very probable con-. clufions as to the defigned continuance of them. a fhepherd may run up a little hut upon the downs without diging for a foun- dation or beftowing any great expence or labor upon it. and when we fee him thus employed, we judge that he defigns it only for a few days or months, at moft, conveni- ence,

ence, and that it is then to be taken down again. but when we observe any person diging deep for the foundation of an house, and employing a great number of hands in laying it and in raising the superstructure, bestowing upon it a great many ornaments, dividing it into several apartments, some for one use and some for another, taking care to make every thing fast and sure, firm and solid, and puting himself to a vast expence of time and thought and labor and money for this purpose, we conclude of course that he has no design of pulling the house down as soon almost as it is built; or at least we should scarce admire his wisdom if he did so. the application of this similitude must needs I think be very easie. " and I will leave it to you, my children, " to draw the argument yourselves, which " I would suggest by it in favor of a future " state; and would now go on to ask you, " whether we may not in your opinion " venture to look upon that eager desire " and expectation of such a state that be- " longs to the mind of man, as being a " plain intimation given us by the great " former of our spirits, that we are indeed " ordained to live in such a state?" we

have

have many other natural defires and appe-ties belonging to us, fuch as hunger and thirft, in relation to the mere animal life and being; a love of truth, a love of noveltie, a delight in great and magnificent objects, a tafte for focietie and friendfhip, conftituting fo many parts in the intellectual and moral frame of man. and for the gratification and indulgence of every one of thefe defires, we find that the gracious author of our beings has in fact made a very plentiful provifion. now the defire of a future ftate feems to be altogether as natural to us as any of thefe. why then fhould we imagine it to be the only natural inclination belonging to us that will be difappointed? it is the moft important of them all. it is that without which the reft would be comparatively of little value. God can as eafily gratify this as any of the other. and why fhould we fufpect his goodnefs in this particular cafe alone, fo fully verified and amply difplayed in all befides? by how much the nobler (*a*) are the powers and faculties of our

(*a*) " The beft way, fays Mr. *Manlove*, to know that the foul is immortal, is to keep its nobleft faculties in due exercife, and then they will fpeak for themfelves." See his *Dif-*

LEC. XIII. our being, so much the more difficult must it be to reconcile the destruction of it either to the goodness or to the wisdom of the deitie. and this is what I meant by the comparative view of these two topics or sources of argument, the nature and attributes of deitie, and the constitution and frame of man. and in particular, the more intense and eager our hopes of happiness hereafter, so much the more improbable is it that the supreme being should not indulge us in the gratification of them; so much the more difficult to account for our being naturally led to entertain any such hope, if this be not designed.

Present dispensations.

But then farther still we mentioned, as you may remember, a third argument in proof of a future state appointed and ordained for man; and which was to be deduced from the condition of man here upon
" earth,

Discourse concerning the Immortalitie of the Soul, c. ix. p. 114. This seems to have been the argument of the ancient Druids. Inter hos Druidæ ingeniis celsiores, ut autoritas Pythagoræ decrevit, sodalitiis adstricti consortiis, quæstionibus occultarum rerum altarumque erecti sunt, & despectantes humana pronuntiarunt animas immortales. *Ammian. Marcell.* l. xv.

earth, or the conduct of divine providence towards him in the present world. "this " world, my good children, has all the " appearance imaginable of a state in " which we are to be trained up and disci- " plined for another. it is a state of edu- " cation. you perceive your own immedi- " ate and earthly parents to be bestowing a " great deal of thought and care upon you " in your present young and tender age, " and that not merely in providing suste- " nance for your animal life, but in form- " ing likewise your minds and manners, " and leading you into the knowlege of " this or the other science or art, which " you can make but very little use of at " present, and can scarce imagine it may " be of what benefit or advantage it can " be to you to be instructed in them. but " do you think that they would be at all " this trouble, if they were sure that you " would not live to be men and women ; " or if they had not the greatest reason to " presume that you would ? now this is " exactly the conduct of providence to- " wards us all. there are many things in " your present state of education under " your parents and teachers, that may per- " haps

Lec. XIII. "haps be somewhat troublesome, tedious, and vexatious to you, and from which you had much rather be excused. but they are designed to answer a good end bye-and-bye in your *future state* of manhood, if it please God to bring you to it; and you yourselves will then be sensible of this." thus God afflicts many good men here upon earth. even to the very latest moment of their lives they are exercised with sorrows of one kind or another; and these are the discipline of heaven for the improvement and perfecting of their virtue. but for what end can we suppose it to be carried on? why so much care taken for the bettering and improvement of their tempers, if after all themselves are to be so soon as by death annihilated? (*a*) so like-

(*a*) Non mihi itaque videtur hæc parva esse causa, quare cum malis flagellantur & boni, quando Deo placet perditos mores etiam temporalium pœnarum afflictione punire. flagellantur enim *simul*, non quia *simul* agant malam vitam, sed quia *simul* amant temporalem vitam: non quidem *æqualiter*, sed tamen *simul*, quam boni contemnere deberent, ut illi correpti atque correcti consequerentur æternam, ad quam consequendam si nollent esse socii, ferrentur & diligerentur inimici; quia donec vivunt semper incertum

likewife many of the bleffings and enjoy- Lec. XIII.
ments of this life are of fuch a kind as to
be naturally fited for the improvement of
the moral temper, and for exciting in our
minds thofe views and affections, that are
in the directeft manner adapted to prepare
us for another and a nobler ftate of being.
God does not only fupplie us with the meat
that is by the nature of it fuitable and convenient with refpect to our bodily health
and fuftenance, but gives us likewife all
things " richly to enjoy" for the culture of
our minds, for the ftrengthening and improvement of our reafon, for the refinement
and exaltation of our virtue. we enjoy
very ample means and opportunities of a
religious nature. we have the bleffed gofpel of Chrift in our hands. and Chrift
came into our world, notwithftanding all
the amazing glorie and dignitie of which
he

incertum eft, utrum voluntatem fint in melius
mutaturi. *Aug. de Civitat. Dei*, l. i. c. ix. where
we fee the pious and judicious father infifting
upon the afflictions which befall good men, as
being a gracious difcipline, intended not only to
promote their own preparation for a future and
immortal ftate, but alfo to have a like influence
even upon the wicked by means of their example exhibited in the fuitable improvement of
them.

Lec. XIII. he was in the heavenly one poſſeſſed, on purpoſe to confer this bleſſing upon us ; a bleſſing purely ſpiritual, and relative to the higher intereſts of our being. but why all this care on the part of heaven in our religious and moral education, if not with a view to ſome other ſtate in which the ends and purpoſes of it are to be completely anſwered ? what father appoints his ſon to be for a certain number of years employed in learning this or that particular art, occupation or profeſſion, but with a view that he ſhould exerciſe and employ himſelf in the ſame, when that period ſhall expire ? but thus our thoughts are naturally led to the chriſtian plan. which, God willing, ſhall be the ſubject of our diſtinct conſideration on the next opportunitie.

LECTURE XIV.

THE three great sources of argument upon that prime subject, the doctrine of a future state, we have already observed to be as follows: first, the nature and perfections of the divine being, his goodness, his holiness, his power and his wisdom; secondly, the inward frame and structure, the mental powers and affections of man himself; thirdly, his condition here on earth, or the conduct of divine providence towards him in the present life. and under each of these heads we have endevored to evince the certaintie of it. but it is of the highest importance to observe in relation to some of the arguments which in treating of these particulars have been insisted upon, that they will be so much the stronger for the farther continuance of our being, after we have enjoyed the felicitie of the heavenly world for thousands of ages, and so on for thousands of ages still, than they are now for the expectation in general of a life to come. such I mean, as those which were derived from the noble powers, faculties,

faculties and affections of the human mind, and from the goodness of the supreme being, and that delight and complacencie which he ever takes in virtue and holiness. these faculties and affections of our minds, the longer they are exercised amidst the bliss and glories of futuritie, so much the more will they be enlarged and elevated, and so much the more capacious will they still be of greater happiness in a farther extended duration of our being. and the longer we exist in the possession of so sublime a felicitie, so much the stronger and more lively proof and demonstration shall we have of the goodness of the supreme deitie, and of the pleasure he takes both in the virtue and in the happiness of his reasonable and moral offspring, so much the more powerfully and feelingly shall we in this particular be convinced; consequently so much the more improbable will it appear, and so much the more unnatural in us to imagine, that he should by the annihilation of our being deprive us of them both. this therefore is one, and a most important one, of those inferences that are to be deduced from the topics that were insisted upon in our last exercise upon this occasion;

occasion; that there is not only a future, Lec. XIV. but an immortal state of being ordained for man. and thus too we are furnished with a noble and in the highest degree satisfying illustration of what has been before insisted upon, in answer to what is sometimes thought so much to militate against the supposed goodness of the supreme being, namely, those calamities and evils of various kinds, which so much perplex and imbitter this present scene of things. we said that all these evils might be graciously and most benevolently on the part of heaven intended to produce a far greater quantitie or sum of good upon the whole, by the happy consequence of them in some other state of being than could otherways have been effected. the realitie of this other state of being has now been evidently evinced. and in that permanent, everlasting scene of existence, the proofs of which have been thus so lately presented to your consideration, what ample space has the divine providence as it were allowed itself, in which to operate after such a manner as to produce these happie and delightful consequences. and thus how gloriously may the divine and sovereign being display the perfection

fection of his benevolence and wisdom to all his creatures even of the human race, that shall be for ever triumphing with unabating ardor and affection in these demonstrations of his eternal love? " what cala-
" mitie or evil can you possibly imagine,
" my good children, to take place in this
" world, be it ever so heavy, ever so ex-
" tensive, ever so lasting, which may not
" in a future state of never-ending exist-
" ence become the matter of exultation and
" triumph on account of the happie effects,
" with which in that state it will appear to
" have been connected as the instrumental
" and producing cause? effects eternal in
" their duration, yet arising out of an evil,
" which on account of its being an evil of
" this life only, must needs have been al-
" together momentarie and transient." the improvement which by means of such afflictions we make in virtue, is a good which is to be carried with us into another world, and will there be existing in our minds, and growing into a still greater good for ever; so that it is, properly speaking, an eternally good effect arising out of a transient and momentarie evil. thus again, it has been often looked upon as a considerable difficultie

cultie in the scheme and dispensations of divine providence, that good men should so frequently be cut off by death in the midst of their days. this, it must be ackowleged, has indeed been often the case. some of the best of men, in all the vigor of their usefulness, and amidst the highest activitie of their pious zeal, have been thus removed from our world. but then you perceive, according to what we have been insisting upon concerning the realitie of a future state, that, though called out of this world, their happiness is going on in another, their virtuous progress is not at all interrupted, but on the contrary by this removal wonderfully facilitated, and in the highest degree befriended. it is a removal unspeakably advantageous to their own moral improvement. and though we cannot indeed but bemoan their absence; yet may we not justly and usefully look upon it as a punishment for the sins of those who are left behind? may it not answer some very valuable purposes in promoting our own seriousness and pietie to be inquiring at least, whether it be or not? and the want of such good men no longer acting that brave and honorable part on earth, should stir up

those

Lec. XIV. those who yet remain among us, to be proportionably more warm and vigorous in pursuing the same honorable measures. this will be highly advantageous to themselves. and when such is indeed the happie effect of a serious consideration employed upon the so early removal hence of men thus honorably distinguished, the benefit to the world may be upon the whole the same as if they had remained with us, their virtue being thus by means of their removal transfused into the minds of others. what an happy thing to himself was Elijah's translation into heaven? at the same time he was scarce missed in Israel, on account of that holy flame which in consequence of his removal was kindled up in the mind of Elisha. but then, then it is, that the decease of good men is the saddest loss, when they leave none at all, or but a very few indeed, that are equally good behind them. for all the forementioned reasons however, particularly on account of that so much greater happiness which they themselves enjoy in consequence, we see that the removal hence of such, even in the prime and vigor of life, cannot justly be considered as carrying in it any objection to the providence of the

the almightie. this would be in effect to object to it, because the virtuous are made happie, which would be a strange kind of reasoning indeed ! but the argument, as you perceive, supposes that they enter immediately upon the happiness of a future state. and surely we must believe it to be altogether as easy to the divine being to carry on the happiness of the virtuous without breach or interruption, as to revive or renew it after a long intervening state of unconsciousness and insensibilitie. and the one being altogether as easily conceived of as the other, which is it, I would ask, that appears most consistent with the ideas we entertain concerning the exuberance and perfection of the divine goodness? or what can be more unnatural than to imagine that the gracious, sovereign being, whose real design towards us is eternal felicitie, should nevertheless grudge us such a comparatively small, but yet in itself interesting portion of happiness, as may be enjoyed between death and the resurrection? it is as if any one should bestow upon us a large and ample fortune for life, and yet grudge us the sustenance or the provisions of a single day ; which we should at least

look

Lec. XIV. look upon as being strangely whimsical and capricious. and the scriptures seem plainly to suppose that all mankind upon their decease have their habitation or lot assigned them either in heaven or hell. but a state of insensibilitie is neither one nor the other; nor is it possible to conceive of any moral ends or uses that can be answered by it. (*a*) whereas

(*a*) And indeed, says Mr. Grove, if we strictly examine the notion of the *utter extinction* of the being, and its *reproduction* after a certain interval of time, it will appear highly absurd to reason; for after it has once ceased to exist, the same *individual* thinking being can never exist more: a new one may be produced exactly like the former, and so may a *thousand* more; but that will not make them all to be the same being; as it would do for the same reason, as any one of them may be the same with *that* which had an end put to its existence some time ago, whether a longer or a shorter, makes no difference. after there has been a gap or separating space of time, nothing can possibly unite the being existing before, and that which exists after into one. and this alone, to those who believe a resurrection, may be instead of a thousand arguments of the soul's not dying with the body; because in that case the resurrection would not be barely *refitting up the body*, that it might be united to *the same conscious principle*, with which it was in union before (and which had never for a moment ceased to exist, and so

might

EXERCISES.

whereas even in the miseries of a future world inflicted by the supremely governing deitie

Lec. XIV.

might have a title to be rewarded or punished, for what was done in a former body) but *producing another conscious principle*; new as to its very *substance*, if the soul be *immaterial*, and *annihilated*; or at least as to *the principle of life and consciousness*, if it be *matter*; which would constitute it a *distinct individual agent*, having no interest in the good or bad conduct of that other; though, perhaps, it resembles it as nearly as one being can another. the reasoning of *Lucretius* here would be just enough. *Nec si materiam nostram conlegerit ætas*, &c. that if time should gather together our materials after death, and after they were reduced into the same situation, life should be superadded, yet would not that signifie any thing to us; any more than it does what beings had been composed of the same stuff before we were born. See his Treatise on a *Future State*, c. viii. §. xi. p. 110—112.

Q. 1. *I have often wondered why there is nothing in the creed of the immortality of the soul, and its state before the resurrection.*

A. 1. The article of *Christ's descent* tells us, that his soul was among the *separated souls*, while his body was in the grave: as he told the thief, that he *should be that day with him in paradise*. 2. The *resurrection* of the *body* is a thing not known at all by nature, but only by *supernatural revelation*, and therefore is an article of mere belief: but the *immortalitie* or *future life of souls*, is a point which the *light of nature revealeth*, and therefore *was* taken both by *Jews* and sober Heathens

LEC. XIV. deitie for crimes that have been committed in this, the defigns of a moral government will Heathens as a truth of common notice: even as the *love of ourfelves* is not expreffed in the *ten commandments*, but only the love of God and others, becaufe it was a thing pre-fuppofed. 3. The *immortality of the foul* is included in the article of the refurrection of the body: for if the foul continue not, the next at the refurrection would be *another foul*, and a new created one and not the fame: and then the body would not be the *fame foul's body*, nor the *man* the fame *man*, but another. who was ever fo unwife to think that God had fo much more care of the *body* than of the *foul*, as that he would let the *foul perifh*, and raife the *body* from the duft alone, and join it with another foul? 4. Very learned and wife expofitors think that the Greek word (Anaftafis) ufed for *refurrection*, indeed fignifieth the *whole life after this, both of foul firft, and body alfo after*, oft in the New Teftament: it is a *living again*, or *after this life*, called, *a ftanding up again*: and there is great probability of it in Chrift's argument with the *Sadducees*, and fome paffages of Paul's, 1 Cor. xv. Baxter's *Catechizing of Families*, c. xxi. p. 154, 155. To the fame purpofe Dr. Clarke. The notion, fays he, of the *foul's immaterialitie* evidently facilitates the belief of a *refurrection* and of a future retribution, by fecuring a principle of *perfonal individuality*, upon which the juftice of all reward or punifhment is intirely founded; but if *thinking* be in realitie nothing but a *power* or *mode*, which inhering in a loofe and fleeting fyftem

will be still advancing towards their final accomplishment, and the perfections of the great God and father of the universe be even by these in the grand result illustrated and displayed to the view of his intelligent creation. " for far be it from you, my
" good children, to imagine that the wicked
" are punished in a future state out of any
" such principle in the deitie as revenge,
" or what we call passion. no; but you
" are to consider such punishments as the
" measures of a wise and benevolent ruler
" or governor in the moral universe." the best earthly sovereign that ever lived never thought it inconsistent with his goodness to punish malefactors; and his subjects would soon have found the dreadful effects of his not doing so (*a*). if you ask whence these

punish-

system of matter, perishes utterly at the dissolution of the body; then the restoring the power of *thinking* to the same body *at the resurrection*, will not be a raising again of the *same individual person*; but it will be as truly a *creation* of a *new person*, as the addition of the like power of *thinking* to a new body *now*, would be the *creation* of a *new man*. See his *Third Defence*, p. 88.

(*a*) It is upon these principles that an ingenious author thus expresses himself in commenting upon a passage in one of Cicero's Orations.
" Tully's

Lec. XIV. punishments of the wicked will arise, or in what it is they consist: I answer; first, in the

" Tully's business in this Oration was to paint
" out Clodius in his true colors, to let people
" see into the hands of what an ill man they
" had given the power of a tribune, to let his
" judges see what a guilty wretch they had ab-
" solved; to convince his whole audience that
" a villain absolved by corrupt judges could
" not yet but be miserable, through the irre-
" gularity of his passions and affections and the
" consciousness of his misdeeds: pursuant to
" this purpose it was proper for him to distin-
" guish between the punishments exacted by
" men, which were sometimes bought off, and
" those inflicted by the Gods, which were
" never to be avoided; the one reaching body
" and goods, the other the mind. The Gods
" interpose not in what concerns the former;
" their inflictions are laid on the mind. self-
" consciousness and reflection are the ministers
" of their vengeance; they make use of no
" other to punish wickedness. This is all that
" Tully says; and many good men, as well
" christians as deists, who believe the future
" state, will say upon the matter the same thing.
" but, though according to Tully, the Gods
" have ordained only self-consciousness and re-
" flection to punish wickedness in this life, may
" they not have ordained this also, though this
" only, to punish it hereafter? I say not ever-
" lastingly, for Tully had other notions of the
" Gods than that comes to; but so long at
" least,

the remorſe of their own conſcience; by Lec. XIV.
this ſome have been even plagued to death
while in this world. and it will be a much
greater ſource of torment in the other, becauſe there will be nothing there to divert
their attention from theſe diſmal reflections,
or to alleviate the pains of a ſelf-accuſing
mind. ſecondly, the worſt of company,
whoſe buſineſs and delight it will be to in-
ſult and deride, to tantalize and torment
them, out of pride and envie. thirdly, a
moſt lively ſenſe of having forfeited the
divine favor, and being in a ſtate of alie-
nation from the beſt of beings. it is oftentimes a matter of no ſmall vexation and
uneaſineſs even here, to think of having by
our own imprudence and folly, forfeited the
friendſhip of ſome wiſe and worthy man.
imagine then, if you can, what a vexation
and torment it muſt needs be to any one in

" leaſt, till the puniſhment ſhall work a change
" of mind in the ſufferer, and then the puniſh-
" ment cannot but ceaſe. I intereſt not myſelf
" in the caſe, but take it for granted that
" Tully could make the Gods authors of no
" puniſhments, but what were deſigned for the
" amendment of the ſufferer, and the inſtruc-
" tion of the beholder." See *Free Thoughts on
a Future State*, p. 45, 46.

O his

Lec. XIV. his most deeply reflecting moments, to be continually accusing and upbraiding himself for having forfeited the friendship of his God! and being now excluded from a sublime and glorious felicitie, which he himself might have been enjoying as well as others, had it not been for his own wilfulness and folly! and by considering only and reflecting upon the direct contrary of all these particulars, you may easily furnish yourselves with some notion or idea, enough to animate all the efforts of your minds, be it only duly attended to, of the happiness of futurity. as dreadful and tormenting as are the agonizing tortures of an accusing conscience, so great, satisfying and delightful will be the pleasures of an approving one; of reviewing and looking back upon our own integritie, and that unshaken fortitude, with which by divine grace we have been enabled to maintain our contest with sin and folly, whether that of our own or others. the greater difficulty, opposition, hazard, fear and despondencie in the progress of our virtue here, so much the more exquisitely joyful will be the reflection of our minds upon having at length and for ever surmounted all. and if we

cannot

EXERCISES.

cannot but look upon it as being the very worſt of evils to be baniſhed from the favorable and propitious preſence of God our maker, and to live under the perpetual, keen and moſt pungent ſenſe of a loſs ſo inexpreſſibly great, we may by this means come to form ſome idea or notion of that intenſe and elevated happineſs, which cannot but be the reſult of a directly contrary ſtate and ſituation, of being the objects of divine complacencie and love, and moſt intimately conſcious of it. and then, thirdly, when we reflect upon the amazing number of other holy, heavenly, virtuous men, who are gone before us into that happy ſtate of being towards which we ourſelves are daily tending, and how many more will follow us thither; what a prodigious company of pure and virtuous ſpirits from every quarter of the univerſe have been, and will be continually reſorting to it, and what a vaſt inconceivable number more there is, who have from the beginning had their reſidence and habitation in it, what an idea muſt this give us of thoſe pleaſures of ſocietie and friendſhip, of harmony, love and union that are there to be enjoyed! nothing however can furniſh us with a more pleaſing ſenti-

Lec. XIV. sentiment of this nature, than our reflecting upon that close, inseparable union, which we shall then have with our lord Jesus Christ himself, the great "author" of eternal happiness to all those, who believe in and " obey him," and the " captain" of our " salvation." " this is he, as an inge-
" nious writer expresses it, will the sepa-
" rate soul then say, who put on our nature
" with its infirmities, but by his resurrec-
" tion and ascension on high, has changed
" his infirmities into glory. this is he,
" who conversed here below in mean con-
" dition among men, and behold him
" raised above the magnificence of all
" the angels. this is he that once suffered
" the *contradiction of sinners*, but receives
" now the applause and veneration of all
" the inhabitants of heaven. this is he
" that ignominiously hung upon a cross,
" but now all creatures behold him with
" reverence and trembling. this is he,
" that here below suffered death, but who
" now holds in his hands the life of all
" things and the substance of the universe.
" this is he that was once seen lying in a
" dark tomb, in comparison of whom now
" the splendor of the sun is but as a shadow.
" this

EXERCISES.

"this is he was thought unworthy that
"the earth should bear him, who now
"walks upon the heavens, and under
"whose feet the whole fabric of the earth
"does tremble. this is he *in whom* I once
"*believed* "only," but whom I now *see*
"fully and manifestly, and to whom I have
"liberty to approche without fear, and
"*behold* him *face to face.*" such then, my
"children, is the notion or idea that
"you are to form of the happiness of
"the heavenly world, and of the rewards
"of (*a*) virtue there to be confered."
and we may easily see the shocking impro‑
prietie there must be in the conduct of any
one, who expecting to participate in so
great and glorious an happiness as this,
should demean himself to the baseness of a
vicious and worldly spirit.

But the reflections now last insisted upon
naturally lead us to what we proposed this
evening to enter upon; the more distinct

Lec. XIV.

Christian revelation,

(*a*) Rewards, which, though they be too
great to be understood by the sons of men, yet
are not so great, but that they may be expected
by us, when we shall be adopted to be the sons
of that God; whose power to bestow, can be
equaled by nothing but by his desire to gratifie.
See Mackenzie's *Moral Paradox*, p. 52.

Lec. XIV. consideration namely of the christian scheme of religion. "and the first question, my
" good children, which naturally offers
" itself upon this head is, what you sup-
" pose to be meaned by christianitie or the
" christian religion? and you will answer
" no doubt, that by christianitie, or the
" christian religion, according to the ap-
" prehension you have entertained, is to
" be understood those doctrines and duties
" that were preached and published in the
" world by Jesus Christ and his apostles,
" Peter, Paul, James and others; the
" knowlege of which doctrines and duties
" are communicated to us in the writings of
" the new testament; and to the truth and
" authoritie of which God has borne wit-
" ness by *signs and wonders and divers miracles*

what. " *and gifts of the Holie Ghost.* so that chri-
" stianitie you are to look upon as a divine
" revelation of religion superadded to the
" original and primarie light of nature in
" relation to it." many of the doctrines of it are the same with those of natural religion. but then they are differently re-veled; namely, by the personal authoritie of our lord Jesus Christ, as the great pro-phet of God, and the miraculous attestations

tions which accompanied his publication of Lec. XIV. them. so that even with respect to these doctrines taught by the light of nature, you are to consider it as being a vast advantage resulting from christianitie, that by means of it an additional and twofold evidence has been given to them. we have their importance by this means more strongly inculcated upon us, and the authoritie and truth of them so much more firmly evinced. and then farther these doctrines of original, primitive and natural religion christianitie has enforced and enlightened, not only by its authoritie as more directly and immediately applied to them, but likewise by a great varietie of doctrines peculiar to itself, supported by the same authoritie; and all illustrating and confirming these great maxims of primitive revelation. " now, my good children, you will easily " perceive that such an additional and spe- " cial revelation of religion as that which " I have been speaking of is *possible*." that Possible, there are other intelligent beings besides ourselves inhabiting other worlds, is a sentiment founded even upon the discoveries and conclusions of nature itself, as we have already in the course of these lectures had

occasion

Lec. XIV. occasion to observe. now it is altogether as easie for the supreme deitie to commission some one or other of these beings to appear in our world, and to take up his abode amongst us for a time, and for the answering such or such a salutarie and useful purpose, as it was for him to appoint any of us our habitation and stated residence here. so that there is nothing that can be in the least degree absurd in supposing that some such being may have appeared in our world in order to publish the doctrines of religion among mankind under the sanction of a distinct and special authoritie for this purpose confered upon him. but how, may some be inclined to say, is his authoritie to be evinced? how are we to be satisfied that he does appear in our world invested with such a divine commission? now this can only be made evident by such miraculous works already hinted at in this view, " by you, my good children;" such extraordinarie, unaccustomed operations, as cannot be accounted for by any apparent powers of nature, and which tend to engage the attention of mankind to the doctrines of such a teacher, and to diffuse the knowlege and reception of them throughout the world,

the

EXERCISES.

the design of which therefore we cannot but suppose to be the pointing him out to us as a special and divine teacher, and the giving success to the doctrines he should deliver. these doctrines we cannot imagine would ever have been in such an especial manner attested, countenanced and supported by heaven itself, were they not in reality both true and of the utmost importance to mankind. nor can any thing be more clear and evident than the possibility of such miraculous events or operations. for the whole system of nature we know to be the workmanship of God. and what more naturally supposable, than that he can cause whatever deviations he thinks proper from the usual course and order of nature, which may constitute so many miracles to us, though an original part in the plan of his universal government, as much as the natural state itself of the world and its events. and to say that the supreme being cannot cause miracles to be performed or to take place, would be as great an absurditie as to say, that he who makes a watch cannot pull it to pieces, or make it go faster or slower as he thinks fit, or suspend its motions, or alter in this manner or that, the form, contexture and workmanship

Lec. XIV. manſhip of it. the continuance of our being is every moment owing to the immediate and inſtantaneous power of the deitie, exerted for the ſupport of it. can it then be doubted, whether that being, by whoſe power millions and millions of creatures are thus in the common and ordinary courſe of nature continued in exiſtence, ſhould not be able, if he thinks fit, inſtantly to heal, or impower another in this manner to heal, the diſeaſes of any among mankind, and ſo to continue and lengthen out their lives ? our very life itſelf we have originally from God. he is the giver and author of it. now muſt we not needs believe that it is altogether as eaſy to him to reſtore life in this or that particular inſtance, if ſuch be his will and pleaſure, as it was at firſt to give it ? can it ever be thought impoſſible to that being inſtantly, if he pleaſes, to ſuſpend the influence of the winds, to whoſe power alone, every moment exerted, it is owing that they have any influence at all ? or that he, to whoſe continued agencie in ſupporting the uſual operations of nature, we muſt needs aſcribe the nouriſhing qualitie of all our food, ſhould be able to communicate it in any other manner he
ſhall

EXERCISES.

shall think proper, and with equal ease, to [Lec. XIV.] a smaller as to a larger portion of it, even in the same degree; or make the bread itself to increase and multiply with as much ease as the grain or seed, from the produce of which it is made. so far then we seem to be upon very certain grounds advanced. but though the possibilitie of such a revelation, as that which is now the subject of our discourse, be indeed a necessary step in the argument, yet must it needs be the lowest. let it therefore be added, that such a revelation is not only possible but highly credible. that is to say, all things considered and duly weighed, nothing can to our reflection appear more *likely*, than that the [Likely.] divine being should, in some such manner as we christians suppose he actually has, revele himself to mankind; at least there can be nothing in such a supposition carrying in it the very lowest degree of improbabilitie; so that we cannot reasonably be surprised at hearing of such a thing. for consider only the prevalence in the world of iniquitie, and the numerous temptations to it; the various afflictions and sorrows of human life, and the need we have of support and comfort under them. consider on the

Lec. XIV. the other hand, the bleffings and joys of a virtuous life, and the vaft, unfpeakable felicitie of making a continual progrefs in it. confider thefe things, I fay, and then judge whether it be not a moft natural prefumption, that a God of infinite benignitie and goodnefs fhould in fuch a manner revele himfelf to us, as to afford us fome additional aid and affiftance in our virtuous progrefs, and for enabling us the better both to encounter the temptations of life, and to bear its ills; and after a manner more fublime and elevated to enjoy the pleafures of virtue and religion. in the fyftem of animal and external nature we find a very kind provifion made for *incidental* wants and diftempers, fuch as men may have brought upon themfelves, or that may have befallen them through the inconfideration, folly or injuftice of others, or by means of any afflictions, which may have come upon them with little or no pre-apprehenfion of any fuch matter, yet without either their own, or the fault of any one befides, as well as for the *ftated* wants of nature, and the infirmities originally belonging to our frame. why then fhould it be thought incredible that God may have furnifhed us with the like

EXERCISES.

like salutarie and graciously intended medicines for our souls infirmities and for the diseases of the mind? that in fact he has done this by the appearance of Christ Jesus in our world, and the nature and qualities of his gracious prescriptions in this kind, shall, God willing, be the business of our next meeting upon this occasion, to evince.

Lec. XIV.

LECTURE XV.

WE have already made it to appear that such a divine revelation as that we suppose to be contained in the gospel, is a thing possible, or what very well may be. we have likewise shewn it to be a thing credible; or that it is at least no way improbable that it should be. the next step in this argument is those ancient prophesies, which for many ages preceding the actual publication of the gospel to mankind, declared that it would be. these prophesies are contained in the writings of the old testament. thus it is that we are to distinguish on account of several, and those very

Lect. XV.

Ancient prophesies.

LECT. XV. very remarkable, predictions, which we meet with in the new. with respect then to those of the old testament, by which the appearance of our blessed savior amongst mankind was prefigured and pointed out, they were intended in the first place for the comfort and entertainment, the satisfaction and joy of those to whom they were originally delivered. this is plain from what you, " my
" good children, may remember our bles-
" sed savior himself to have declared con-
Abraham. " cerning Abraham, who lived so many
" ages before the coming of Christ into
" our world, that he *saw his day and was
" glad.* what do you think can be the
" meaning of Abraham's *seeing Christ's
" day?* it must surely mean his foreseeing
" in consequence of a divine revelation
" that had been given him for that purpose,
" that at such an appointed time some il-
" lustrious messenger from heaven would
" appear among men, would assume the
" character of a savior, and in a most glori-
" ous sense and in an absolutely complete
" and perfect manner fulfil it. well therefore
" may it be added that he *was glad.* and
" let me more particularly observe it to you
" by the way, that this joy of his must
" needs

" needs have been of the benevolent kind;
" it flowed from a generous, public spirit,
" and the delight he took in the common
" good and general welfare of his brethren
" of mankind. the moſt diſtant poſteritie
" he conſidered in that light. and there-
" fore he rejoiced in Chriſt's day for the
" ſake and in behalf of thoſe, who after
" ſo long a ſucceſſion of years, were to
" enjoy the benefit and light of it. and
" this I mention in order to ſhew you, that
" it is to be one exerciſe of your benevo-
" lence and friendſhip towards mankind to
" be pleaſed and delighted with whatever
" good is befalling any of your fellow-
" creatures, whether it be by means of your
" own endevors or thoſe of another; or
" whether it be in the courſe and order of
" divine providence, without the interven-
" tion of any human inſtrumentalitie at
" all. nay, as the inſtance and example
" before us does indeed ſo particularly ſig-
" nifie and point out, you are not only to
" *rejoice with them that do rejoice,* but even
" with them that ſhall rejoice, when you
" can have any probable or certain pre-
" apprehenſion of it."

Such

Lect. XV. Such was the case of Abraham with respect to gospel-times or the christian revelation. for these prophesies, this knowlege communicated to him concerning these far distant events must needs have been miraculous. it was altogether as impossible that he should know of these things so long beforehand without a miracle, as that without a miracle the sick and dying should be instantly healed, or the dead raised to life. and by whom can we suppose such extraordinary and special knowlege to have been communicated to any of mankind, but by that supreme being himself, who has " kept " the times and seasons within his own " power," and from whom alone therefore it could procede? when therefore it was in this manner declared unto Abraham, " that " in his seed all the nations of the earth " should be blessed"; that is, in and by Christ Jesus, who was to descend from him, he might most certainly depend upon the truth of it; such a miraculous and special revelation of this far distant event being properly speaking a divine promise; the promise of a *God that cannot lie.* " observe " that, my good children, God is a being " that *cannot lie.* from whence you may
" most

EXERCISES.

"most certainly infer that you ought not
"to lie, or to deceive another. for you
"are *to be perfect as God your father who is
"in heaven, is perfect.* and God *cannot* lie;
"because he is a being so perfect in the
"moral excellencie of his nature, as that
"he can never be disposed to it, so that
"the more like you are to God, the less
"prone you will be to lying; the more
"you will abhor it. at the same time you
"know how expressly it is made incumbent
"upon you by the sacred scriptures, that
"you be *followers of God as dear children*."
But with respect to the prophesies we have been speaking of, they were ever and anon renewed; Moses had the foreknowlege of Christ's coming communicated to him from above as well as Abraham. and there are many of the psalms containing prophetical descriptions of his appearance and character; several of which are to be known by those quotations which are made from them as prophesies by our blessed savior and his apostles. by this means we learn that the second, twenty-second, and the hundred and tenth psalms contain prophesies of this kind, being refered to in this view by the writers of the new testament. but in those books

LECT. XV. books of the old which we particularly
style prophetic, though they predict many
other future events, and contain a great
varietie of inftructions and admonitions ad-
dreffed to thofe of the then prefent times,
it is that we meet with the greateft varietie
of clear and moft remarkable defcriptions
given of our bleffed favior, of the nature
of his kingdom and the defign of his appearance. witnefs only the fifty-third chapter of Ifaiah, in which we have a defcription fo exactly anfwering to what our favior
did and taught and fuffered, whilft here
upon earth, which muft very much furprife
you, when you confider that it had been
exhibited fo many ages before he actually
appeared. amongft men. "and yet you are
" not to imagine, my good children, that
" this is fo furprifing as not to be believed ;
" for we ourfelves, you and I and others,
" often foretell things to come ; that is to
" fay, we inform this or the other friend,
" that on fuch or fuch a day, a week or a
" month or two hence, we defign to do fo
" or fo, or to be at fuch or fuch a place ;
" and accordingly it very often fo comes to
" pafs tho' not always, becaufe we are apt
" to change our minds, or providence may
                          " prevent

" prevent our doing that which we still
" defign to do. now God knows all things
" from the begining even to the end, fu-
" ture as well as paft. and as with him
" there is no *variablenefs or fhadow of turn-*
" *ing*, whatever he defigns will certainly
" come to pafs, it not being in the power
" of any other being to prevent the execu-
" tion of it. and certainly whenever he
" thinks proper he can communicate to
" any of his creatures a knowlege of fuch
" defigns, and caufe them in prophetic
" language to be exhibited. for, it would
" be ftrange indeed that he, who has given
" us all our knowlege and our very capa-
" citie for knowlege and of communicating
" it to one another, fhould not himfelf be
" able to communicate it to us in this par-
" ticular branch or fpecies of communica-
" tion, as well as in any other way. fo
" that there is in realitie no more difficultie
" in apprehending that *God at fundry times*
" *fpake unto the fathers by the prophets* con-
" cerning Jefus Chrift, than there is in
" apprehending that one man may com-
" municate his intentions to another." and
furely it anfwered a very good purpofe as
already intimated. it was fetting before the
men

Lect. XV. men of those times a very pleasing and delightful prospect, and might afford in this respect the highest entertainment; the foresight of these glorious times being by no means confined to the person by whom the prophecy was originally delivered. others, who were credibly informed of it might safely depend upon its accomplishment, as well as he; so that every age would enjoy the benefit of those which had been delivered in that preceding, and as the number of them increased, their confidence in the accomplishment of the event would be so much the more confirmed. on all these accounts then we may justly say that christianitie was proved even before it had a being in the world; these prophesies being so many attestations given to it, as properly speaking, miraculous, as any of the miracles themselves recorded in the gospel. and then secondly, if they proved christianitie even to those who lived before the appearance of Christ in the world, and who could not have had it proved to them in any other way, they must certainly constitute a very great accession or increase of evidence in favor of it in these times succeding his appearance. for they are still prophesies and miracles

miracles still; and by a diligent and proper consideration of them our idea of the evidence and proof attending it cannot but be prodigiously heightened and enlarged. *(a)*

LECT. XV.

But now farther, fourthly, as it is possible that such a revelation as that we supposed to be contained in the gospel might be given to mankind, as there is nothing improbable in supposing that it should, as it was foretold for many ages before that such a revelation would be communicated, so accordingly in the course and order of divine providence, and at the time appointed for it, this has actually been done. for the illustration of this particular there are four things to be considered, and to one or other of these heads every thing relating to the more direct and immediate proof of christianitie may properly and naturally be reduced. first, the character of its author; secondly, the nature and tendency of the doctrines which he taught: thirdly, the miracles by which these doctrines were attested and confirmed: and, fourthly, the manner

---

(a) χρεία δὲ τῶν προκαταγγειλάντων αὐτῷ τὴν παρουσίαν πρὸς βεβαίωσιν τῆς αὐτῶ παρουσίας, ὅτι προκατήγγελτο. *Epiphan. Adverf. Heref.* Lib. ii. Vol. i. p. 696.

Lect. XV.

Moral character.

manner in which the knowlege of these things have been conveyed down to us. first then, with respect to the character of its author: this is a point of very high and considerable moment, not only on account of the example exhibited, but in relation more directly to the proof of his divine authoritie. nothing can be more unlikely than that the supreme deitie should commission any being of an immoral character to treat with mankind upon the great subject of religion and a future life. there would be such an inaptitude and incongruitie in this case between the message and the messenger, as would by no means harmonise with the beautie of the divine conduct in other respects so apparent to mankind; so that from hence alone suspicions would very naturally arise as to the realitie of the message. just in the same manner as if in common life any of us were to receive a pretended message from some friend of ours by a person to whom it appeared very improbable that he should commit such an affair. the very character of the person would lead us to suspect a fraud. besides, one who plainly enough discovered himself to be of a corrupt disposition in other instances,

stances, we might naturally enough suppose to be guilty of a design to impose upon us a pretended revelation; so that whatever such a person delivered, however excellent in itself, under the notion of a divine and specially reveled doctrine, and whatever seemingly strong attestations it might be attended with, still it would gain but little credit on account of those perpetual suspicions which we should be apt to entertain of some intended mischief lurking under these fair appearances, founded upon the immoral character of him assuming the prophetic office. supposing his message to be really divine, these suspicions would nevertheless take place. consequently the employing any one of such a character on the part of heaven in a message of this nature to mankind, would be a defeating of the very end proposed. he would be sent " that he might be believed on in the " world." and yet, notwithstanding all his credentials, the badness of his character would naturally tend to prevent that belief. it is not therefore consistent either with the goodness or the wisdom of the divine being, that the author of such a revelation should be of a character like this. and on the other

LECT. XV. other hand, if any one declares himself to be such a divine prophet, and appeals to a great varietie of miraculous works by him performed in proof of that claim, and if at the same time he appears throughout the whole of his conduct to be a person, not merely of an inoffensive, but of an highly useful character, full of generosity, kindness, meekness, pietie and undaunted courage in the cause of God and goodness, we immediately conclude, that, if God did indeed in any such manner discover and make known his will to mankind, it would surely be by the mediation or intervention of a person thus characterized and distinguished. and from the goodness of his character in all other respects, we should naturally be led to look upon it as so much the more improbable that he should act the part of an impostor in relation to the message, which he declares himself to have been commissioned from above to deliver. but if in this case the character be not only highly excellent, but absolutely complete and perfect, the credibilitie of the prophetic claim is by this means prodigiously heightened. we see here an evident connexion between his example and his doctrine;

EXERCISES.

trine, which has all the appearance of being a regular and orderly scheme. they mutually enforce each other; and there is such an aspect of contrivance, wisdom and design in this as naturally betokens a realitie, and amounts to a very strong presumption of truth in the case. "now, my good
" children, these observations which we
" have last been making, are no other
" than a representation of the real cha-
" racter of our lord Jesus Christ. he was
" a person, not only inoffensive, but in
" the highest degree pious, benevolent and
" friendly in all his actions. his character
" was not only an excellent, but an abso-
" lutely perfect one. he was surrounded,
" you know, with enemies, who were
" always upon the watch against him,
" in order to find out if possible, some-
" thing unfavorable, something unpopu-
" lar, something odious and malignant to
" fasten upon him, but they could never
" do it. they could not *convince him of*
" *sin.* he himself, notwithstanding all their
" malice, challenged them to do so. you
" see then, that of all persons that have
" ever appeared in our world, he was
" the most likely, on account of his own

" imme-

"immediate character, to be the author of a divine revelation to mankind, and the special minister of divine grace and mercy for our recoverie and salvation. and therefore when you find him actually to make this claim, you may the more readily assent to it. these things agree and harmonise so well as to be a natural ground of belief in the instance of such a claim advanced." and now as to the second point or article in this argument; the nature and tendencie of the doctrine delivered by our savior. it is a doctrine calculated to promote the highest good of men both here and hereafter. it teaches meekness and quietness, contentment and patience, to do good and to bear evil. it presents to the mind the most pleasing and delightful truths and contemplations. it recommends, and actually supplies us with, that knowlege, which is of all others the most useful and entertaining. it is intended to make us like God, and consequently to advance us to the truest and most sublime felicitie of our own beings. it gives us the most amiable views of the divine nature and providence, and thus chears and supports our minds under the afflictive dispensations

EXERCISES.

fations of the prefent life. all thefe things it inculcates not only fo far, and upon the fame principles, as did the light of nature; but likewife by a great varietie of difcoveries that are peculiar to itfelf. difcoveries in relation to things, of which without it we could not poffibly have had the leaft notion or idea. every thing that it delivers to us concerning Jefus Chrift himfelf (*a*) and the Holy Spirit, and a great many

Lect. XV.

Tendency of

(*a*) The prodigioufly high degree of moral force and energy accompanying thefe difcoveries, fo far as relates to the perfon, character and offices of our lord Jefus Chrift, will perhaps better appear from the following foliloquy than by any formal modes of argumentative illuftration. "o fweet
" Jefus! o amiable lord! whither through ex-
" ceffive grief I fhould turn mine heart, I know
" not; when I confider what abject and bitter
" things thou haft undergone for my fins. and
" who can be of fo cold and obdurate an heart,
" that this love of our redeemer does not in-
" flame? to the end that he might deliver us
" from the pains to which we were liable thro'
" fin, himfelf fuffered the pains due unto fin.
" o moft merciful God! what fhall we render
" to thee for this thine unfpeakable grace and
" charitie! we formerly, indeed, admired much
" that thou wouldft vouchfafe to debafe thyfelf
" fo far, as to take our human nature upon
" thee, to be born in a ftable, to be laid in a
" manger;

L̲ECT. XV. many particulars in relation to the heavenly world are peculiar to this difpenfation; as alfo the inftitutions of baptifm and the lord's fupper, both of them fo admirably fited for cherifhing and invigorating the divine and heavenly life within us. (*a*) and all

" manger; but when we confider the humilitie
" of thy paffion, in which thou difdainedft not
" to be contemned and trampled upon like a vile
" worm of the earth, we even faint away thro'
" admiration." *See* Meditations upon the Paffion of our Lord and Saviour Jefus Chrift; fet
forth by J. C. London, 1695. p. 42, 43. " this
" being fo, as we have it expreffed, *ibid.* p. 102,
" 103, how is it poffible we fhould ever forget
" this immenfe charitie? it is truly a wonder
" our hearts are not wholly diffolved in the love
" of him. it is a wonder we can ever ceafe
" from praife and thankfgiving! how can we
" confent to love any thing befides him, whofe
" excefs of love is fo great towards us? how can
" we entertain any other thoughts or cares than
" to return love for love? why do we refufe to
" fuffer for his fake, who fuffered fo much for
" ours? how comes it to pafs we fcarce vouch-
" fafe even to *think* of what he fo willingly
" acted and endured for us? o moft fweet Jefu!
" what piety overcomes thee? what charity
" hath vanquifhed thine heart, that for us moft
" vile finners, thou fhouldft undergo fo bitter
" and ignominious a paffion?"

(*a*) " The bread indeed, fays an ancient
" writer, is meer food alone, but there is in it
" never-

all these things do in a wonderfully pleasing and delightful manner concur to raise
our

" neverthelefs a life-giving power." fo like-
" wife with refpect to baptifm; "a mere outward
" ablution is not the thing intended; but that
" by the power of the water operating in a
" way of lively faith and active hope in a due
" performance of the facred rite; and by means
" of the holy names employed, it may become
" perfective of our falvation." βρῶσις μὲν ὁ ἄρτος,
ἡ δὲ δύναμις ἐν αὐτῷ εἰς ζωογονήσιν. καὶ ὐκ ἵνα τὸ
ὕδωρ ἡμᾶς καθαρίσῃ μόνον, ἀλλ' ἵνα ἐν τῇ ἰσχύϊ τῦ
ὕδατος διὰ τῆς πίςεως, καὶ ἐνεργείας, καὶ ἐλπίδος,
καὶ μυςηρίων τελειωσέως, καὶ ὀνομασίας τῆς ἁγιαςείας,
γενήλαι ἡμῖν εἰς τελείωσιν σωτηρίας. *Epiphanii* Ana-
cephal. Op. Vol. II. p. 154. it is on account
of fuch excellent effects arifing from the due
celebration of thefe ordinances, as well as the
illuftrious character of the great inftitutor of
them, that St. Bafil, fpeaking of baptifm in
particular, calls it *moft glorious* baptifm, and
moft admirable baptifm. ἐνδοξοτάτου βαπλίσματος
—&—τῦ θαυμασιωτάτου βαπλίσματος. De Bap-
tifmo, L. I. c. ii. Op. Vol. I. p. 643. what,
fays the pious archbishop Leighton, was that
other facrament (baptifm) and this (the Lord's
fupper) but coverts, under which Chrift conveys
himfelf and his graces to the *believing* foul,
while the prophane and flight-hearted are fent
away with empty elements. See his eighteen
Sermons, N° 8. p. 135. to the fame fenfe, fo far
as relates to the holy fupper, we have a learned
catechift expreffing himfelf. A. *qualis autem ea*
debet

Lect. XV. our conceptions of the majefty and goodnefs of the divine being, to make us more in love with religion and virtue, to infpire our hearts with a fervent charitie, and to produce the greateft truft and confidence in the almightie lord and governor of the univerfe. fo that in fhort, chriftianitie is exactly fuch a fyftem of religion as we might naturally fuppofe, and moft probably prefume a divinely authorifed teacher and inftructor of mankind to introduce, if ever fuch an one fhould really appear. and confidered in this view the doctrine of chriftianitie goes a great way towards proving itfelf. when a perfon lays claim to a divine commiffion for teaching a doctrine like this, and

debet effe commemoratio ? B. non tantum hiftorica, in fummis aut labris aut cerebro fluida (quæ hypocritarum & maxime impiorum effe poteft) fed *practica* & *affectuofa*, quæ vim quandam falutarem animæ *fideli* alte imprimit ac infigit. A. *id explica uberius.* B. talis effe debet Chrifti in cœna fua recordatio, quæ 1°. *crucifixi* domini amoris erga fe melitiffimo fenfu participantis animum pafcat, & cœlefti voluptate perfundat. 2°. quæ amoris viciffim erga Chriftum igniculos in corde communicantis exfufcitet, & in illius laudes meritiffimas & obfequium rapiat. 3°. quæ charitate flagret in *proximum*, maxime in domefticos fidei: *Tullii* Enchirid. p. 130, 131.

EXERCISES.

and works miracles in proof of it, againſt which there is no exception lying, as to the truth and realitie of them, how can we heſitate about the admiting of ſuch a claim or embracing the doctrine? what obſtruction or impediment can there be to our aſſent? but this leads us to the third particular mentioned in this argument; namely, the miracles of the goſpel, as wrought both by our ſavior and his apoſtles. theſe were very great and numerous. they were wrought in the moſt public manner imaginable. they were very different in the kind and ſpecies of them, and for the moſt part ſuch as upon the very firſt view and appearance of them we cannot but conclude to be abſolutely above the powers of nature, and beyond the utmoſt reach of human ſubtletie, art or contrivance. ſuch as the healing at a diſtance and in a moment; and raiſing the dead to life. the miracles in theſe ſeveral kinds were repeted again and again. and there was always a great number of our ſavior's enemies at hand, who would have been glad, if they could, to have detected him in any fraud; and who had all the opportunitie they themſelves could deſire of doing this, had there been

Lect. XV.

Miracles.

occa-

occasion given in the nature or the manner of the performance; and yet it was not done. " now, my good children, I think you will easily apprehend, that if a person takes upon him to work miracles, and declares that he does so, and affords others the fairest opportunitie for examining into the truth and realitie of them, and if vast numbers at the very time and place, when and in which these miracles are said to have been wrought, are quite eager to lay hold of this opportunitie, and to examine into the truth of them with the greatest strictness and accuracie, and if these very persons would have been beyond measure glad to have found that they were not true and genuine miracles, and yet after all this examination declare them to be true and genuine, as our savior's enemies did with respect to those that were performed by him, you must needs think and believe them to be so; you must see surely the necessity of admiting them as such, if you would act like rational beings. and, if upon such evidence we are not to believe, I know not how we can rationally believe any matter of fact at all." we have already observed too that prophesies are

are a species or a distinct sort of miracles; and of this kind there are several, as has before been intimated, which we meet with in the New Testament as delivered by our blessed savior and his apostles. the destruction of Jerusalem, for example, was foretold by our savior himself, according to what we find recorded in the twenty-fourth chapter of St. Matthew, the thirteenth of St. Mark, and the twenty-first chapter of St. Luke, in so great a varietie of plain, expressive, distinguishing particulars, as are not capable of being applied to any other event, but exactly answering to that. so that, as it is plain that our savior in what is recorded by the several evangelists in those chapters, did indeed design to deliver a prophesie, it must needs too be evident that it could be no other than a prophesie of the destruction of that city; which did accordingly, and in the manner there described come to pass. so likewise the apostles foretold the appearance and establishment of poperie in the christian world so many hundred years before it took place; an event so extremely improbable in itself, that it could never enter into any man's imagination to forge a pro-

Lect. XV.

New Testament prophesies.

a prophesie of that kind. and, if it had, it is scarcely possible he should have hit upon so many circumstances of similitude as are apparent between poperie as now actually existing in the world, and poperie as we have it described by St. Paul and in the book of revelation. now all these prophesies (*a*) and miracles have in fact given the highest credit and authoritie to christianitie, insomuch that by means of them, as was naturally to be imagined, the whole world in a manner has been led to the knowlege of it. " and can you, my children, believe that God should by such extraordinarie methods of his providence teach men a falshood ?" but this leads us

(*a*) It is to be observed too, that as prophesie does thus strongly enforce the authoritie of the christian religion in general, so is it naturally corroborative of the doctrine of a future state in particular. this is ingeniously urged by Erasmus. quid multis ? quum omnia sic evenerint quemadmodum erant prædicta, de supremo judicio, deque piorum & impiorum præmiis quicquam addubitare videtur esse extremæ cæcitatis. homini divino credimus, si ter quaterque verum prædixit : & ei quam in tam multis, tamque juxta sensum humanum incredibilibus, fuit veridicus, non credemus in uno quod restat ? *In Symbolum*, cap. v. p. 198, 199.

us to reflect, in the fourth place, upon the manner in which the knowlege of these things has been conveyed to ourselves. now it is an undeniable fact, that such a vast number of converts as we have just now been speaking of, were actually made by the preaching of the gospel. and yet it was a religion, which for a great number of years after its first publication, no man could profess without exposing himself to great sufferings and dangers, and even to death itself. for the sake of it however, notwithstanding all these dangers, such the vast, amazing number who renounced the principles in which they had been educated, which had all the force and authoritie of all the kings and princes and priests of the earth in favor of them ; and christianitie all this force and weight of authoritie against it. so that it appears utterly impossible to account for the conduct of these primitive converts to the christian faith, without supposing that there were really such miraculous atteftations given to it as out-weighed all these temporal and political confiderations. for there were no temporal or political confiderations on the other fide, that could effect it. either

Lect.XV.

Historical

Attestation,

there-

LECT. XV. therefore chriftianitie muft be true, or here is a great palpable event, a permanent appearance in the world which we are not able any way to account for, but for which, fuppofing chriftianitie to be true, the moft natural and obvious reafons may be affigned. befides, through a vaft number of writings that have been publifhed to the world fince the time when it is faid to have been firft made known down to the prefent age, the knowlege of it is in fact to be traced and obferved, according to the account given of it in the New Teftament. in every age we find chriftianitie, and meet with it in hiftorie, owned and acknowleged among mankind, juft in fuch a manner as we muft fuppofe, admiting the writings of the New Teftament to be authentic. out of which writings there are in the ancient books of this kind, a vaft number of quotations exactly anfwering to fuch and fuch paffages now to be met with in that book; and thefe paffages are quoted as from authors of undoubted credit and authoritie. this therefore proves two things, both that the evangelifts and apoftles were looked upon as credible writers, and that their writings have been faithfully and truly tranfmited

down

down to our times. and they all of them
assert the miracles of Christ, and the authoritie of what he declared, delivered and made known to mankind. the latter follows of course from the former, and of the former they were very capable judges. many of them were actually eye-witnesses of these miraculous performances, and the rest lived at the very time, and on the very spot where these miracles were wrought, and had the best means of knowing whether they were true and genuine miracles or not. and these very preachers of christianitie exposed themselves to every imaginable difficultie and suffering for the sake of it. what should induce them to do this, if they did not believe it to be true? " you
" do not, my good children, see men now
" a-days exposing themselves to pain and
" tortures and povertie and death itself
" for nothing; and yet the apostles did so,
" unless christianitie be true. for there is
" nothing else but the truth of that doc-
" trine, which could have induced them
" to act the part they did. this then you
" may conclude, that it is a *faithful*, that
" is a credible and well-attested *saying*,
" *and worthy of all acceptation, that Christ*
" *Jesus*

LECT. XV. "*Jesus came into the world to save sinners.*
"you may not perhaps enter at present
"into the force of all that I have been
"saying upon this head, or be able to re-
"collect it exactly. but I hope that it
"may be the means of exciting your
"curiositie hereafter to enquire a little
"into these things, and even of leading
"you to apprehend at present that there
"is some good reason to be given for that
"reverence with which we desire you to
"be attending to those instructions that
"are given to you in the bible; and if
"any thing of this kind should happily
"be effected, I shall have obtained mine
"aim: this at least I hope you will con-
"clude, that I do for mine own part ap-
"prehend, that there is a very sure foun-
"dation for the belief and principles of
"religion; so that you may depend upon
"it for the future that I am greatly in
"earnest when I call upon you to be and
"to do good, to *live soberly, righteously and*
"*godly in this present world,* to love devo-
"tion, prayer and the public worship of
"God, and to *search the scriptures.* nay,
"though you should forget every thing
"that I have said, yet thus much I hope
                                                            "you

EXERCISES.

" you will remember, that I used to come
" to you from time to time, and employ
" myself in endevoring to convey some
" useful instruction into your minds. and
" this will put you upon asking your pa-
" rents, or others that may be able to in-
" form you what it was that I was used
" then to discourse about. this I can af-
" sure you of, that I shall always reflect
" with pleasure upon the part I have borne
" in this evening exercise, out of the real
" concern that I have for your best interests
" and highest good, and from the hearty
" wish of my soul, that you may be a *seed*
" *to serve the lord, and be accounted unto him*
" *for a generation*; that you may not any
" of you be a *grief to your father, or a bit-*
" *terness to her that bare you*, but that you
" may be to them as *olive-plants around*
" *their table*, and like the pleasant vines or
" fragrant flowers of the garden."

THE END.

Lately published by the Author, *and printed for*
J. Johnson, *in* St. Paul's Church-Yard

DISCOURSES on the PARABLES and MIRACLES of Our BLESSED SAVIOR, in Four Vols. Octavo. Price sewed 1l.

www.ingramcontent.com/pod-product-compliance
Lightning Source LLC
Chambersburg PA
CBHW021154230426
43667CB00006B/399